CONSUMER REPORTS

MUTUAL FUNDS
BOOK

CONSUMER REPORTS

MUTUAL FUNDS

BOOK

GREG DAUGHERTY

and the Editors of
Consumer Reports Books

CONSUMER REPORTS BOOKS
A Division of Consumers Union
Yonkers, New York

Copyright © 1994 by Consumers Union of United
States, Inc., Yonkers, New York 10703.

Published by Consumers Union of United States, Inc., Yonkers, New York 10703.
All rights reserved, including the right of reproduction in whole or in part
in any form.

Library of Congress Cataloging-in-Publication Data
Daugherty, Greg.
    Consumer Reports mutual funds book / Greg Daugherty and the
editors of Consumer Reports Books.
        p.   cm.
    Includes index.
    ISBN 0-89043-723-8
    1. Mutual funds.   I. Consumer Reports Books.   II. Title.
HG4530.D38   1994
332.63′27—dc20   93–42317
                                                                                   CIP

Material appearing on pages 16 and 17 copyright © 1989 by Peter Lynch. Reprinted by
permission of Simon & Schuster, Inc.

Design by GDS / Jeffrey L. Ward

First printing, April 1994

This book is printed on recycled paper. ✪
Manufactured in the United States of America

Consumer Reports Mutual Funds Book is a Consumer Reports Book published by Consumers Union, the nonprofit organization that publishes *Consumer Reports,* the monthly magazine of test reports, product Ratings, and buying guidance. Established in 1936, Consumers Union is chartered under the Not-for-Profit Corporation Law of the State of New York.

The purposes of Consumers Union, as stated in its charter, are to provide consumers with information and counsel on consumer goods and services, to give information on all matters relating to the expenditure of the family income, and to initiate and to cooperate with individual and group efforts seeking to create and maintain decent living standards.

Consumers Union derives its income solely from the sale of *Consumer Reports* and other publications. In addition, expenses of occasional public service efforts may be met, in part, by nonrestrictive, noncommercial contributions, grants, and fees. Consumers Union accepts no advertising or product samples and is not beholden in any way to any commercial interest. Its Ratings and reports are solely for the use of the readers of its publications. Neither the Ratings, nor the reports, nor any Consumers Union publications, including this book, may be used in advertising or for any commercial purpose. Consumers Union will take all steps open to it to prevent such uses of its material, its name, or the name of *Consumer Reports.*

For Sheila, Megan, and Bob

Acknowledgments

I would like to thank my friends at Consumer Reports Books, in particular Mark Hoffman for his careful editing, and Ruth Turner and Sarah Uman for their support and encouragement. Thanks also to my colleagues at *Consumer Reports* magazine: Marge Frohne, the late Bob Klein, Irwin Landau, Trudy Lieberman, Bill McGuire, Tobie Stanger, and Moye Thompson. Thanks to Cindy Callison, Joe Mansueto, and Jackie Swift at Morningstar, Inc., for their tireless work on the Ratings; and to Warren Boroson for his insightful comments on an early draft of this book.

Contents

CONSUMER REPORTS

MUTUAL FUNDS

BOOK

INTRODUCTION

The goal of this book isn't to sell you on a specific mutual fund, a particular family of funds, or even on mutual funds in general. Its goal is to make mutual funds as understandable as possible for people who want to invest their money productively, but who don't want to make investing their life's work.

This book will not try to persuade you that you should enjoy reading a mutual fund prospectus—but it will try to make reading the important parts of a prospectus easier. It will not make you feel guilty for failing to chart your funds' prices on a daily basis—but it will show you ways to keep track of your funds so you don't lose sight of them entirely.

Consumer Reports has been rating funds periodically since the early 1980s. During that brief time, we have seen boom and bust, and periods when it was difficult to know *what* was going on. We believe that mutual funds are good investments for most people. By that we mean good mutual funds—the kind this book will show you how to find.

Here, to get started, is a quick overview of what the chapters in this book will cover.

Chapter 1, The Basics of Mutual Funds, describes what funds are and compares them with other common types of investments.

Chapter 2, Which Funds Are Right for You?, looks at the different varieties of funds and shows how to decide whether a fund's goals are in keeping with your own.

Chapter 3, Where and How to Buy Fund Shares, explains how to buy a mutual fund, details the various fees to watch out for, and presents a simple system for buying shares more economically.

Chapter 4, How to Build a Portfolio of Funds, shows how to select a diversified portfolio of mutual funds based on your age, your goals, and your tolerance for risk.

Chapter 5, Mutual Funds for Retirement Planning, explains how to use mutual funds to save for retirement and to live more comfortably during your retirement years.

Chapter 6, Taxes and Mutual Funds, describes the tax implications of both taxable and tax-free mutual funds.

Chapter 7, When and How to Sell Fund Shares, offers strategies for cashing in your fund shares at the best possible times and prices.

Chapter 8, Getting Good Service from Your Fund, details the services that mutual fund "families" offer their investors and explains how to switch from one fund to another within a family.

Chapter 9, Consumer Reports Ratings of Mutual Funds, features our most recent Ratings of stock and bond funds, along with a commentary on how to understand and use fund performance data.

The glossary of common mutual fund terms translates the financial jargon you'll encounter in reading about mutual funds into plain English.

We hope you find this book readable, practical, and (above all) profitable.

1 THE BASICS OF MUTUAL FUNDS

WHAT IS A MUTUAL FUND?

A mutual fund is a company that pools money from many individual investors to buy a large portfolio of financial assets. Those assets might include stocks, bonds, and other, more exotic securities. Investors receive shares in the fund in proportion to the size of their investment. The value of those shares will rise and fall in step with the assets in the fund's portfolio.

There are two basic types of funds: open-end funds and closed-end funds. Open-end funds sell and buy back shares to meet investor demand. Closed-end funds issue a fixed number of shares, which then trade on stock exchanges, much as stocks do. The price of a closed-end fund's shares fluctuates to reflect not only the value of the assets it holds, but also the demand for the fund's shares. This book concerns itself primarily with the more common, open-end variety of mutual funds, but closed-end funds will be touched on where appropriate.

WHY INVEST IN FUNDS?

Fund companies are fond of touting three advantages that mutual funds are said to have over other types of investments. And, indeed, there is

3

some truth behind the touting. Those three advantages are the following:

1. Diversification. When you buy a share of a mutual fund, you receive a slice of its entire portfolio. That portfolio may, for example, own stock in hundreds of different companies. If the stock of one of those companies should tumble in value, the damage to the total portfolio will be minimal. However, if you happened to own shares of that stock outside of a mutual fund, it would presumably represent a much greater portion of your portfolio. In that case, the damage to your personal portfolio could be far more serious.

While diversification is an undeniable advantage, it doesn't protect you from every possible danger. For example, when the stock market as a whole declines, most stocks may fall in value. A diversified portfolio may lose just as much of your money as an undiversified one. It may even lose more.

2. Professional management. Fund companies also like to boast of the skills and resources they can bring to the job of managing a portfolio. For many investors, the prospect of having a full-time manager looking after their money is the major selling point of funds. That's particularly true if the fund manager is known to have had a string of highly profitable years.

During the fund boom of the 1980s, in fact, some fund managers became celebrities of a sort, with name recognition to rival that of TV game-show hosts or minor pop singers. Peter Lynch, the manager of Fidelity's Magellan Fund, was a figure of such renown that his decision to retire in 1990 at age 46 was national news. Lynch's retirement also created a dilemma for thousands of Magellan shareholders: Should they trust their money to the fund's new manager or cash in their chips? Those who stayed on faced a similar dilemma when, two years later, Lynch's successor departed and yet another new manager took the helm.

But as has been demonstrated time and again, today's "hot" fund manager can be tomorrow's laggard. So rather than get caught up in the personality cult of fund managers, choose a fund that has performed well in relation to other funds of its type over a significant period of time, whether under one manager or several. (The Ratings in chapter 9 show how.)

If you learn that the manager of a fund you own has been replaced, you may want to keep an eye on your fund's performance for a time to see if the new manager is doing as well as the old one was. If the new manager turns in a consistently poor performance, compared with other funds with similar investment objectives, you may want to move your money into a different fund.

One type of fund, called an index fund, neither benefits from good managers nor suffers from bad ones. Rather than employ a manager to decide which securities to buy and sell, index funds simply buy whatever securities make up a particular index, such as the well-known S&P (Standard & Poor's) 500 stock market index. The theory behind index funds is that since few fund managers consistently beat the indexes year after year, an investor might do better simply to "buy" the index itself. Index funds may never be top performers, but they tend to do at least as well as the average fund of their category. They also benefit from having lower operating costs to pass along to investors than actively managed funds.

3. Liquidity. Liquidity is a measure of how fast you can convert an asset into cash. A checking account, for example, is very liquid; you can get your money out at any time. A house or family business, on the other hand, is far less liquid; either may take months or even years to sell.

Most mutual fund accounts are nearly as liquid as a checking account at your bank. Shares are easy to buy and sell. You don't have to find a seller when you want to buy shares or a buyer when you're ready to sell them. The fund itself will sell you shares or buy them back. Often, all it takes is a phone call. Some funds will also allow you to write checks against your account to redeem shares.

Unlike a bank checking account, however, the balance in your mutual fund account will fluctuate on a daily basis, depending on the value of the fund's portfolio of assets. So you may pay more for shares you buy on one day than on another day, or you may get more money for a share you sell on one day than on another. (We'll look at some smart strategies for buying and selling in later chapters.)

FUNDS VERSUS OTHER INVESTMENTS

Try as fund salespeople and some financial writers might, it's difficult to generalize about how mutual funds are likely to perform compared with other types of investments. For one thing, all mutual funds are not alike.

Any two funds may invest in entirely different things. One fund may be managed well, another poorly. And the economic forces that favored one investment over another in a given year may prove fickle in the years that follow.

Nevertheless, understanding the relative merits of different types of investments can help you make better choices. Here's a look at how mutual funds stand up against their most common competitors for your investment dollars.

FUNDS VERSUS BANKS

Banks have one clear advantage over mutual funds: Bank accounts are federally insured. Unless your accounts exceed the limits of that insurance (currently $100,000 per account), you are unlikely to lose a cent of the money you keep in the bank. With mutual funds, you could theoretically lose your entire investment, although that's very unlikely. For a mutual fund to lose all of its value, every single security it owns would have to become worthless.

The clear disadvantage of keeping your money in the bank is that your rate of return is likely to be far less, over time, than the potential return on stocks, bonds, and other types of investments. The following chart puts that in perspective. It shows how much money you would have accumulated if you had invested $2,000 a year from 1988 through 1992 in several different investments.

As you can see from the chart, putting $2,000 a year (a total of $10,000 over five years) into bank certificates-of-deposit (which pay more interest than bank checking or savings accounts) would have resulted in an accumulation of $12,183. The same investment in corporate bonds would have grown to $14,090. In stocks, it would have grown to $15,440. Bear in mind, of course, that you can also lose money in stocks and bonds, while bank accounts preserve your principal.

Bank certificates-of-deposit also are less liquid than mutual funds shares. You generally can't cash in a CD before its maturity date without having to pay penalties.

To keep depositors from leaving the bank altogether, many banks now offer mutual funds. (We'll look at that phenomenon later in this book.)

HOW INVESTMENTS HAVE PERFORMED

The bars below show how much money you would have if you had invested $2000 a year for each of the years 1988 through 1992 in stocks (as represented by the Standard & Poor's 500) and some other common investments. Bear in mind that these were relatively good years for both stocks and corporate bonds. Stocks, in particular, may lose money in any given year.

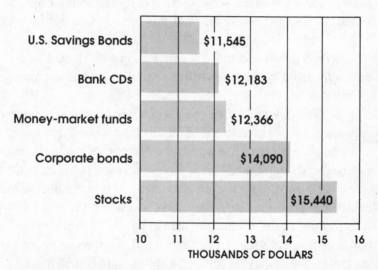

Sources: Bank Rate Monitor, U.S. Treasury Department,
*   IBC/Donoghue's Money Fund Averages, Lehman Brothers*

FUNDS VERSUS U.S. SAVINGS BONDS

Many people's first foray into investing begins with the purchase of a U.S. Savings Bond. Children are often introduced to bonds as gifts from their parents or grandparents.

Like mutual funds, U.S. Savings Bonds are easy to invest in. Many employers offer both mutual funds and savings bonds as part of their payroll-savings programs. Such programs make regular investing virtually effortless once you've signed up for them.

Series EE Savings Bonds currently (1994) pay a variable rate of interest based on the rate paid on U.S. Treasury securities. They also promise to pay a minimum rate of interest if you hold on to them long enough. At this writing, if you keep a bond at least five years, you'll earn the higher of 4 percent (the guaranteed rate) or 85 percent of the average yield on five-year Treasury securities (the variable rate). Because they're safe and relatively predictable, savings bonds can be an attractive alternative to bank certificates-of-deposit. Long-term, however, their return is far below that of stocks and corporate bonds. Consulting the chart on page 7, you'll see that a series of $2,000 investments in savings bonds would have done even worse than the same investment in bank CDs: $11,545 versus $12,183.

Savings bonds also suffer in comparison with mutual funds when it comes to liquidity. You can't cash one in until you have owned it for six months.

In their favor, savings bonds are government-guaranteed and require very small investments. Just $25 buys a bond that will be worth $50 when it reaches its full face value. Because their interest rate varies, savings bonds don't attain their face value on a predictable date; they continue to earn interest even after they reach face value. Some companies' payroll-deduction plans accept investments of just a few dollars each pay period toward the purchase of bonds. The interest that savings bonds earn is not subject to state or local income tax. Federal income tax on the bonds may be deferred until they are cashed in.

FUNDS VERSUS INDIVIDUAL STOCKS

Many mutual funds invest in stocks, either entirely or for part of their portfolio. By buying stocks in the form of a mutual fund, you gain the advantage of diversification. If the fund's portfolio manager is a skillful stock-picker, you also benefit from his or her investment expertise.

Mutual funds can be an economical way for small investors to participate in the stock market. Stockbrokers generally charge larger commissions on purchases of less than 100 shares of stock (called "odd lots") than they do on purchases of 100 shares, or multiples of 100 shares (called "round lots"). To buy 100 shares of a $30 stock would require an investment of $3,000 plus commissions. Mutual funds typically require initial investments of $1,000 to $3,000, and many allow later investments of $100 or less.

Individual stocks, however, have at least one advantage over mutual funds for investors with the money and knowledge to invest in them: That's a savings at tax time. Mutual funds constantly buy and sell stocks, and they return your share of any profit to you as a capital-gains distribution. Capital gains are taxable for the year you receive them. But if you own individual shares of stock and simply hold on to them, you won't owe any tax on your capital gains until you finally sell.

FUNDS VERSUS INDIVIDUAL BONDS

Funds that invest in bonds have portfolios that consist of many different issues. That diversification insulates bond-fund investors from some of the risks that buyers of individual bonds must live with.

One of those perils is called "credit risk." If one of the major bond-rating services downgrades a particular bond's credit rating, the market price of that bond will drop. (A credit rating is a judgment of the bond issuer's ability to repay its debts.) That can be a problem if you own an individual bond and need to sell it before it reaches its maturity date. In an extreme example of credit risk, the company or government that issued a bond may default on its debts, making that bond virtually worthless. Because bond funds are widely diversified, the credit problems of any single bond issuer are not likely to have a major effect on the value of their shares.

Like stocks, individual bonds are expensive to buy in small quantities. At a minimum, you may have to invest $5,000. Many bond funds, by comparison, require minimum initial investments of only $1,000 to $3,000 and allow subsequent investments of $100 or less.

Individual bonds have at least one potential advantage over bond funds: predictability. Most individual bonds pay a set rate of interest twice a year until they mature. Unless your bond is "called" (that is, redeemed prematurely) by its issuer, you'll receive that interest for as long as you own the bond. Because bond funds' portfolios are constantly changing, the amount of interest they pay can vary—up or down. Bond funds do, however, pay interest monthly, which can be more convenient than the twice-a-year payments of individual bonds if you need the income from your investments to pay monthly living expenses.

FUNDS VERSUS ALL THE REST

As we'll explore in later chapters, there are mutual funds that invest in virtually anything you could invest in on your own, including foreign stocks and bonds, gold, real estate, and mortgage-backed securities. As a general rule, the more difficult an investment would be for you to buy, to keep track of, and finally to sell on your own, the more investing in it through a mutual fund makes sense.

BEFORE YOU INVEST IN FUNDS

Just as it's possible to make money in mutual funds, it's possible to lose money. So before you invest in funds, make sure you have money set aside to cover your family's expenses in case you lose your job or face a financial emergency. Most of that emergency fund belongs in a safe place, such as a federally insured bank account or a money-market fund.

Consumer Reports' advice over the years has been for households to try to set aside enough money to cover six months' worth of essential living expenses. Two-income couples may be able to make do with three months' worth, assuming they both don't lose their jobs at the same time.

Having an adequate emergency fund established before you begin investing is wise for two important reasons: One, you may actually face an emergency at some point and need the money. Two, you'll spend far fewer sleepless nights worrying about your mutual funds if you know you're investing for the long term and can afford to ride out the inevitable downturns.

A BRIEF HISTORY OF MUTUAL FUNDS

The mutual fund as we know it today is largely an American invention, but its roots reach back to Scotland in the early 1870s. Wealthy Scottish merchants, unhappy with the money they could make by investing in Great Britain, looked abroad for better prospects. They found them in the United States, a nation still rebuilding after a calamitous civil war. Because the United States was so hungry for investment capital, its government securities and railroad bonds were paying nearly twice the rate of interest as similar securities in Britain.

The Scottish merchants bought shares in investment trusts, a forerunner of the modern mutual fund. The trusts, in turn, invested the merchants' money in a diversified portfolio of American bonds. Much of that money went toward building the U.S. transcontinental railroad system.

Coming to America

There is some dispute among financial historians about when the investment trust concept finally immigrated to the United States. But by the 1920s, trusts were flourishing. More than 700 investment trusts and investment holding companies were formed between 1927 and 1930. Of those, 265 were launched in a single year, 1929.

The year 1929 was memorable for another reason: In October the stock market crashed. From their peak prices earlier in 1929 to their lowest point in the Great Depression year of 1932, stocks lost nearly 90 percent of their value. Trust investors saw the value of their shares fall just as dramatically, in some cases even more so.

The New Deal of the 1930s brought long-overdue reforms to the securities industry, and the mutual fund as we know it today was born. The Securities Act of 1933, the Securities Exchange Act of 1934, and most pertinent for mutual funds, the Investment Company Act of 1940, put an end to many of the risky and, in some cases, dishonest practices that had contributed to the 1929 crash.

The term "mutual fund" seems to have emerged in the late 1930s, though its precise origin is hard to pin down. One credible theory is that it was invented in order to give fund salespeople a friendly new name for their product. Terms such as "investment trust" and "investment pool" reminded too many Americans of the fortunes they'd lost in the crash.

The Postwar Boom

After the end of World War II, mutual funds became a way for Americans to invest in their country's postwar prosperity. In 1945 mutual funds collectively held about $1 billion in assets, a figure that would multiply many times over in the prosperous 1950s and 1960s. By the early 1970s, their collective assets had surpassed $50 billion—partly the result of a rising stock market and partly because of the aggressiveness with which they were sold.

The end of the 1960s also marked the end of the postwar fund boom. A prolonged stock market decline in 1969 and 1970 dampened many investors' enthusiasm for stock funds—particularly the new "performance funds" that used risky investing techniques to increase their returns. Though 1969 was hardly as bleak as 1929, the well-publicized beating that some funds took that year was enough to scare off some investors for years to come.

The 1970s brought two innovations: the money-market fund and the tax-free fund. Money-market mutual funds invest in a portfolio of very short-term government and corporate securities. They generally pay a higher rate of interest than bank accounts, with little added risk. Money-market funds caught on quickly and introduced a new generation of small investors to the concept of mutual funds. Tax-free funds, which invest in municipal bonds, pay income to their shareholders that usually isn't subject to federal income tax. Both money-market funds and tax-free funds opened up opportunities to small investors that once had been reserved for large businesses and wealthy individuals.

The 1980s marked another giddy period for mutual funds. Funds began the 1980s with $95 billion in assets and ended the decade with 10 times that amount. Even in 1987, a year best remembered for its stock market crash, investors put more money into mutual funds than they took out.

In the early 1990s, as this book is being written, the mutual fund industry is still growing rapidly. Part of the reason is that banks are paying low rates of interest on deposits, so people are looking for other places to put their money. That, in turn, has compelled many banks to get into the mutual fund business.

If there's one vital lesson to be learned from the history of mutual funds, it's that funds have always had their ups and downs—and probably always will. Neither good times nor bad ones are forever. Booms, alas, eventually come to an end. Busts, thankfully, tend to do likewise.

Note: For readers interested in more of the history of mutual funds, *The Story of Investment Companies* by Hugh Bullock (Columbia University Press, 1959) is a valuable guide and a source for much of the preceding account. For more recent histories of the financial landscape, the books of John Brooks and of Robert Sobel, though only partly focused on mutual funds, are useful references and surprisingly good reading.

Inside Information

One good source of information on mutual fund investing is the fund industry itself. Several trade groups publish educational material for fund investors, much of it basic enough for novices. Don't expect hard-hitting comparisons of fund performance or bold exposés of industry shenanigans. Do expect readable information at a very reasonable price.

The Investment Company Institute, the oldest and largest of the groups, represents more than 3,700 fund companies and related businesses. It publishes an annual Directory of Mutual Funds (current price $8.50) and a variety of brochures and other materials. For information, write:

Investment Company Institute
P.O. Box 27850
Washington, DC 20038-7850

The Mutual Fund Education Alliance is an association of 32 fund companies that sell shares directly to the public. It publishes a directory, The Investor's Guide to Low-Cost Mutual Funds (current price $5), twice each year, in January and July. The association also offers other educational materials for fund investors. For information, write:

Mutual Fund Education Alliance
1900 Erie Street, Suite 120
Kansas City, MO 64116

The 100% No-Load Mutual Fund Council is an organization of 40 management companies that collectively offer more than 160 pure no-load funds. ("Pure" no-load funds don't impose sales charges, long-term redemption charges, or annual 12b-1 fees.) This group publishes an annual Investment Guide and Member Fund Directory (current price $3). For information, write:

100% No-Load Mutual Fund Council
1501 Broadway, Suite 1809
New York, NY 10036

2 WHICH FUNDS ARE RIGHT FOR YOU?

The futurist Alvin Toffler popularized a word some years ago that aptly describes today's mutual fund marketplace. That word is "overchoice." Consumers now can choose from among an almost overwhelming number and variety of mutual funds. At this writing, there are more than 4,000 funds available to investors, with new ones being launched all the time.

In many ways, of course, the ever-expanding universe of mutual funds should be good news for consumers. In theory, more choice means more competition among fund companies and a greater chance to find a fund (or set of funds) that precisely fits your needs.

But how to go about it? Like many problems, the one of choosing the right fund is easiest to solve if broken into manageable pieces. This chapter divides mutual funds into practical categories. Early in the description of each fund category, we describe what types of people, with what kinds of goals, a fund in that category might be right for. Then, we describe the people it is probably wrong for. That's followed by a brief description of what the funds invest in and how they tend to perform relative to other types of funds.

Each category ends with a short list of top performers from *Consumer Reports'* 1993 Ratings that more or less fit that particular mold.

We say "more or less" because categorizing funds is a slippery business. Any two rating services may assign a given fund to different categories. The fund may put itself in still another category—sometimes because its recent performance will make it appear to be a standout in that group, while it would merely be an also-ran in the other ones.

Don't limit your search strictly to our short lists of top performers. Other funds may be more appropriate for your particular needs. (For the names of more funds in each category, see the Ratings in chapter 9.)

To help you negotiate your way through the mutual fund maze, we will cover the following basic categories:

1. Stock funds
2. Bond funds
3. Tax-free municipal bond funds
4. Index funds
5. Mortgage-backed funds
6. Real estate funds
7. International and global funds
8. Sector funds
9. Precious-metals funds
10. "Ethical" and "socially responsible" funds
11. Asset-allocation funds
12. Money-market funds
13. Closed-end funds
14. Funds that invest in other funds

1. STOCK FUNDS

A stock is a share of ownership in a corporation. The first mutual funds in the United States, launched back in the 1920s, were stock funds. In 1976 there were 278 stock funds in operation, with assets of roughly $32 billion. By 1993 there were more than 1,300, with assets exceeding $595 billion.

More than any other type of mutual fund, stock funds illustrate two of the advantages of investing in mutual funds. First, there's diversification. A stock fund may own dozens, perhaps many hundreds, of different stocks; if one of the stocks owned by a fund becomes worthless, that won't be a fatal blow to the fund's overall portfolio. By contrast, a small investor whose portfolio happened to include that ill-fated stock could be badly hurt.

The second advantage is active, professional management. Fund managers relieve the individual investor of having to make decisions on what stocks to buy and when to sell them. Managers aren't always right, of course, and sometimes they are disastrously wrong. But the time and resources they can bring to the job give them a definite edge over the average small investor.

Of course, you can't just put your money in a stock fund and forget about it. Nor should you invest in just any fund. Some funds are consistently better managed than others, and even the good ones can lose their way. The advice in chapter 3 on buying a fund and the Ratings in chapter 9 can help you in choosing a stock fund with a long record of solid management. Chapter 7 can help you decide when the time has come to sell a fund.

Why Invest in Stocks?

In October 1987 the stock market lost more than 24 percent of its value in just a few days—the most memorable of which, October 19, came to be known as Black Monday. Many investors vowed never to buy stocks—or stock mutual funds—again.

Less vivid than the memory of the 1987 crash is what happened in the years that immediately followed. In 1988 the market, as measured by the S&P 500, gained 16.5 percent. In 1989 the market was up 31.7 percent. Investors who held on to their stocks or stock funds after the crash were well rewarded.

Indeed, despite market downturns and the occasional crash, stocks have proven to be good investments over the long term, as any stockbroker or fund salesperson will happily tell you. Peter Lynch, former manager of the Fidelity Magellan fund, the top-performing stock fund in *Consumer Reports'* 1987 Ratings, made the case for stocks in his 1989 book *One Up on Wall Street.* Since 1927, Lynch noted, common stocks had gained an average of 9.8 percent a year, compared with 5 percent for corporate bonds, 4.4 percent for government bonds, and 3.4 percent for Treasury bills. He added, "The advantage of a 9.8 percent return from stocks over a 5 percent return from bonds may sound piddling to some, but consider this financial fable. If at the end of 1927 a modern Rip van Winkle had gone to sleep for 60 years on $20,000 worth of corporate bonds, paying 5 percent compounded, he would have awakened with $373,584—enough for him to afford a nice condo, a Volvo, and a haircut; whereas if he'd invested in stocks, which returned 9.8 percent a year, he'd have $5,459,720."

Lynch, of course, assumes that his sleepy investor had his eyes open wide enough to choose companies that would still be around 60 years in the future. He may also have ignored the tax consequences of van Winkle's investments, in order not to overcomplicate his little fable. And van Winkle would have had to have been pretty well-off to begin with; $20,000 went a long way in 1927. Yet Lynch's point remains valid.

Of course, looking back 60 years can do little for today's investors (beyond making them wish their parents or grandparents had had the foresight, and the cash, to load up on stocks). A more contemporary comparison, for the five-year period 1988 through 1992, would yield the following results:

	AVERAGE ANNUAL RETURN
Common stocks	16%
Corporate bonds	11
Government bonds	10
Treasury bills	6

That five-year period, it's worth noting, was an unusually good one for stocks—and for bonds, as well. And persuasive as those figures may be, they still beg the most important question of all: What will stocks do in the future?

The answer: Who knows? But this much can be said. If the U.S. economy continues to grow in the years ahead, the owners of stocks and stock mutual funds should benefit from that growth. If the economy doesn't grow or, worse still, if it withers, then all of us, investors and noninvestors alike, could face serious economic problems. There is no such thing as a risk-free stock market investment, but a well-diversified stock fund can reduce the risk somewhat.

Six Basic Types of Stock Funds

For convenience, the six categories we use here are the same ones found in the Ratings of mutual funds in chapter 9. They are based on investment objective and listed alphabetically: aggressive-growth, balanced, equity-income, growth, growth-and-income, and small-company. At the end of the section on stocks, some other types of funds that don't readily fit into any of those six categories are discussed.

Aggressive-Growth Funds

For: Long-term investors with strong nerves. If you're investing for a far-off goal, such as a newborn's college tuition or your retirement, aggressive-growth funds may be an appropriate investment, at least for a portion of your portfolio. If they perform as intended, their returns should outpace those of more conservative types of stock funds over the long haul.

Not for: The squeamish—or investors who might need to withdraw their money in the near future, say in a year or two. You should definitely avoid them if you're shopping for a fund that will provide current income. (In that case, look instead to an equity-income fund or to one of the many varieties of bond funds, discussed later in this chapter.)

How they work: The objective of aggressive-growth funds is maximum capital gains. For that reason, they tend to invest in promising new companies or in old companies whose stock prices have been beaten down but seem poised for a comeback. The managers of these funds don't concern themselves with dividend income. They may also use riskier trading techniques than more conservative funds do, such as option writing, short selling, and buying on margin. (For definitions of these techniques, see "Option," "Selling short," and "Margin account" in the glossary.)

In theory, aggressive-growth funds should compensate investors for the greater risks they take by eventually delivering better returns than stock funds in general. Yet a study by Morningstar, Inc., the firm that provided performance data for *Consumer Reports'* most recent fund Ratings, seems to contradict that theory. It found that in a 10-year period ending in August 1992, the group of 22 aggressive funds it studied had average annual returns of 11 percent, compared with average annual returns of 14 percent for growth-and-income funds, which tend to be much more cautious. The study also found that only two of the aggressive funds beat the S&P 500 stock index over that 10-year period. One plausible explanation is that the sharp decline of interest rates in the 1980s benefited conservative funds more than aggressive ones, a pattern that may not repeat itself anytime soon.

Of course, past performance isn't a perfect predictor of what aggressive-growth funds—or any type of fund—will do in the future. So an aggressive-growth fund may belong in your portfolio anyway, if you are willing to take the risk. (See chapter 4 for some suggestions on building a portfolio.)

Frequently, grouped under the general category of aggressive-growth funds are funds that invest in small companies. They are also referred to as small-capitalization, or "small cap," stock funds, which are discussed later in this chapter.

The following aggressive-growth funds (listed alphabetically) were top performers in *Consumer Reports'* 1993 Ratings of stock funds. An asterisk (*) indicates the fund doesn't charge a load (commission) when you buy or sell shares. Average annual returns are for the years 1988 through 1992.

	AVERAGE ANNUAL RETURN
AIM Constellation	23%
*Founders Special	20
Kaufmann	34
*Strong Discovery	21

Balanced Funds

For: Investors looking for modest growth and lower risk to their capital than more aggressive stock funds may offer.

Not for: Investors hoping for spectacular long-term returns.

How they work: Balanced funds try to build a portfolio that strikes a balance between stocks and bonds, hence their name. Since bonds may do well when stocks are faring poorly, and vice versa, balanced funds insulate their owners from the perils of owning just one or the other. At least that's the theory. The trade-off, obviously, is that a balanced fund is unlikely to do as well as a stock fund when stocks are booming or as well as a bond fund when bonds are making great gains.

Though short on thrills, balanced funds are also short on spills. Many of them have been around a long time, and their managers have seen just about everything the financial markets can dish out. The Vanguard/Wellington Fund, for example, was launched in 1928 and has been a solid performer almost ever since.

Even investors whose goals are aggressive and long-term might want to look at a balanced fund with a good record as a way of lending some stability to their overall portfolio. (See chapter 4 for more suggestions on building a portfolio of mutual funds.)

The following balanced funds (listed alphabetically) were top performers in *Consumer Reports'* 1993 Ratings of stock funds. An asterisk (*) indicates the fund doesn't charge a load when you buy or sell shares. Average annual returns are for the years 1988 through 1992.

	AVERAGE ANNUAL RETURN
*CGM Mutual	14%
*Fidelity Balanced	13
Kemper Investment Total Return	15
MainStay Total Return	13

Equity-Income Funds

For: Investors looking for regular income, some growth potential, and less dramatic ups and downs (especially downs). Equity-income funds are among the most conservative types of stock funds. If you're retired and depending on your investments to pay living expenses, an equity-income fund can be a worthy alternative to a bond fund. An equity-income fund can also be a good choice for investors looking for a fairly tame fund to lend a little stability to an otherwise bold portfolio.

Not for: Investors looking for substantial long-term gains or to beat the market.

How they work: If aggressive-growth funds are intended to be the hares of stock funds, equity-income funds are the tortoises. As their name implies, equity-income funds invest in stocks (equities) that pay dividend income. By nature, companies with relatively high, predictable dividends tend to be big, old, and established. The share prices of such companies don't swing wildly, either up or down, except in rare instances. An equity-income fund is likely to own stocks of many such companies. Even if one of them does happen to plummet or soar, it is unlikely to affect the value of the fund much one way or the other.

Equity-income funds can also be a sound choice during uncertain economic times. As evidence of that, not a single equity-income fund in *Consumer Reports'* Ratings received a below-average score for its performance during the 1987 stock market crash. That makes sense for a couple of reasons. One is that the stodgy stocks these funds invest in tend not to appreciate very rapidly, so they don't have as far to tumble when the market falls as a whole. Another is that in turbulent times, many investors take refuge in relatively safe, dividend-paying stocks. That helps keep up the prices of the stocks that equity-income funds own.

Bearing a strong resemblance to equity-income funds are funds known simply as "income funds." The primary difference is that while equity-income funds generally focus on dividend-paying stocks, at least for the bulk of their portfolios, income funds hunt for income wherever they can find it. For that reason their portfolios may contain a mix of dividend-paying stocks, preferred stocks, bonds, short-term notes, and other income-producing securities.

The following equity-income funds (listed alphabetically) were top performers in *Consumer Reports'* 1993 Ratings of stock funds. An asterisk (*) indicates the fund doesn't charge a load when you buy or sell shares. Average annual returns are for the years 1988 through 1992.

	AVERAGE ANNUAL RETURN
*Invesco Industrial Income (formerly Financial Industrial Income)	18%
Shearson Premium Total Return B	17
*USAA Mutual Income Stock	15

Growth Funds

For: Long-term investors willing to accept the usual risks of the stock market—and then some.

Not for: Investors likely to need their money back soon. Growth funds, like aggressive-growth funds, are subject to price swings, so if you're forced by circumstances to sell out when prices are depressed, you, too, could wind up depressed.

How they work: The line between aggressive-growth funds and plain growth funds is blurry. Some funds that call themselves growth funds may, in fact, follow the very strategies and invest in much the same stocks that their aggressive-growth counterparts do. But they may shun the aggressive label for fear it will scare off potential investors.

In general, though, growth stock funds tend to invest in companies that are somewhat larger and better established than those favored by aggressive-growth funds. But like aggressive-growth funds, their objective is capital gains, so they pay little notice to stocks whose primary appeal is dividend income.

A good growth fund can be the centerpiece of a long-term investor's portfolio. It can also lend some growth potential (and inflation protection) to a more conservative portfolio of funds.

Closely related to growth funds (though some bear an even stronger family resemblance to aggressive-growth funds) are capital-appreciation funds. As their name implies, capital-appreciation funds set their sights primarily on stocks with rapid growth prospects rather than those with high dividends.

The following growth funds (listed alphabetically) were top performers in *Consumer Reports'* 1993 Ratings of stock funds. An asterisk (*) indicates the fund doesn't charge a load when you buy or sell shares. Average annual returns are for the years 1988 through 1992.

	AVERAGE ANNUAL RETURN
*Berger 100	24%
Fidelity Blue Chip Growth	19
Fidelity Contrafund	26
MainStay Capital Appreciation	20

Growth-and-Income Funds

For: Investors who want some stocks with growth potential in their portfolios, but who aren't comfortable with the risks associated with aggressive-growth or growth stock funds. Also, investors who want current income but are willing to accept a bit less than an equity-income or bond fund might provide, in return for some growth potential. All in all, growth-and-income funds can be appropriate for almost any investor's portfolio.

Not for: Investors with the single-minded goal of either capital gains or current income.

How they work: Growth-and-income funds invest primarily in a portfolio of well-established stocks—some with growth potential, others that can be counted on for reliable dividend income. In effect, they have two portfolios: one for growth, the other for income. On a continuum of risk, they fall almost smack in the middle between aggressive-growth funds and equity-income funds.

Despite their middle-of-the-road approach, or perhaps because of it, growth-and-income funds have been among the most successful types of funds for investors in recent years. A study cited earlier in this chapter, in the discussion of aggressive-growth funds, found that growth-and-income funds as a group actually outperformed aggressive-growth funds over a 10-year period. That trend may not continue into the future, of course, but it is a strong argument for making one of these funds a central part of your mutual fund portfolio.

The following growth-and-income funds (listed alphabetically) were top performers in *Consumer Reports'* 1993 Ratings of stock funds. An asterisk (*) indicates the fund doesn't charge a load when you buy or sell shares. Average annual returns are for the years 1988 through 1992.

	AVERAGE ANNUAL RETURN
AIM Value	21%
*Clipper	16
Fidelity Growth and Income	18
*Neuberger & Berman Guardian	19
Vista Growth & Income	31

Small-Company Funds

For: Investors looking for long-term growth of their capital—and willing to take a good deal of risk to get there.

Not for: Investors who want regular income from their fund and can't afford potentially large short-term losses.

How they work: Like aggressive-growth funds, these funds aim for rapid growth of capital. They do it by investing in small, usually young companies with what the funds' managers judge to be bright growth prospects. Many of the stocks they buy are not listed on stock exchanges, but are traded "over the counter" on a computerized network maintained by dealers. Small-company stocks, as a group, don't always rise and fall in tandem with larger stocks. The large-stock market, as measured by the S&P 500, for example, may enjoy a stellar year, while small stocks remain in the doldrums. The opposite can also happen. So owning shares in a fund that invests in small companies, along with a fund that invests in larger ones, can give a portfolio some added diversification.

The following small-company funds (listed alphabetically) were top performers in *Consumer Reports'* 1993 Ratings of stock funds. An asterisk (*) indicates the fund doesn't charge a load when you buy or sell shares. Average annual returns are for the years 1988 through 1992.

	AVERAGE ANNUAL RETURN
Alger Small Capitalization	27%
*Robertson Stephens Emerging Growth	23
*Twentieth Century Ultra	26

Note that the third fund on our list, Twentieth Century Ultra, no longer characterizes itself as a small-company fund, but now invests much of its money in medium-size and large firms. The lesson there is that funds can change their strategy over time, sometimes dramatically. For that reason, it's always a good idea to find out what a fund is currently investing in before you buy shares. And if a fund you already own changes course, you need to take a fresh look at whether it is still an appropriate investment for your goals.

Other Types of Stock Funds

Some funds are hard to wedge into any particular category. A good example is IAI Regional, the fund that topped *Consumer Reports'* 1990 Ratings of stock funds. We called it a growth fund because capital appreciation was its stated objective, but its approach is decidedly unusual. IAI Regional invests at least 80 percent of its portfolio in companies headquartered in seven Upper Midwest states—Minnesota, Wisconsin, Iowa, Nebraska, Montana, North Dakota, and South Dakota. The fund, based in Minneapolis, apparently figures that it can choose stocks more effectively if it doesn't stray too far from its own backyard. In *Consumer Reports'* 1993 fund Ratings, IAI Regional was again among the best performing growth funds, though not at the very top.

Other, more specialized types of stock funds will be discussed later in the chapter. Among them are the following:

· Many of the index funds invest in the stocks that make up a sampling of the stock market.

· Real estate funds invest in, among other things, the stocks of companies with large real estate holdings or that stand to profit from homebuilding.

· International and global funds invest in the stocks of foreign (and sometimes American) companies.

· Sector funds specialize in the stocks of certain industries, such as health care or transportation.

· Precious-metals funds own the stocks of mining companies.

· "Ethical" and "socially responsible" funds own stocks of companies that meet certain investors' moral and/or socially conscious criteria.

· Asset-allocation funds invest in a variety of securities, a substantial portion of which may be stocks.

· Closed-end funds may hold a general or highly specialized portfolio of stocks, such as those that trade on one foreign stock exchange. Unlike the other types of mutual funds discussed above, closed-end funds have a fixed number of shares and are traded like stocks.

2. BOND FUNDS

Bonds, simply defined, are the IOUs of corporations, governments, and government agencies. Generally, they pay a fixed rate of interest for a specified term, such as 10 years. At the end of that term, they return the investor's initial investment, called the principal.

Funds that invest in bonds and other types of fixed-income securities represent an even bigger slice of the mutual fund marketplace than stock funds do. In 1993 there were more than 1,600 bond funds available to investors. Collectively, their assets exceeded $580 billion.

Why Buy Bonds?

Investors buy bond funds for good reasons—and for bad ones. One good reason is that bond funds can supply regular monthly income to people, such as retirees, who depend on their investments for support. For many people in that category, owning shares in a bond fund is far more convenient than holding individual bonds. For one thing, individual bonds can be difficult—and expensive—to buy in small quantities. Many bond funds, however, have initial investment minimums in the $1,000 to $3,000 range and later investment minimums of $100 or less. Bond funds also tend to pay their interest monthly, whereas many bonds pay it only twice a year. Finally, many bond funds allow shareholders to write checks against their accounts. That way, shares can be redeemed as needed to pay bills (though not without tax consequences, as explained later in the book).

Another good reason to buy a bond fund is that bonds and stocks (and the funds that specialize in them) perform differently under different economic conditions. Even if your goal is long-term growth of the sort that, historically, only stocks have been able to deliver, you may want to have some money in bond funds as insurance against a prolonged stock market slump.

Those are some of the good reasons to buy a bond fund. What are the bad reasons? Many investors own bond funds simply because they believe (or were told by an eager fund salesperson) that bond funds are safer investments than stock funds. In the short run, that may be true. Yet, over time, bond funds have generally not done as well as stock funds, as the annual returns cited in our earlier discussion of stocks demonstrate.

Worse, some investors have been sold on the belief that "high-yield" bond funds are safe but lucrative places to put their money. High-yield bonds are more commonly known as "junk bonds"—and many of them have lived up to their name. Junk bonds are issued by companies deemed too risky by the financial markets to sell conventional bonds. To compensate investors for the extra risk, the issuers of junk bonds must promise them a higher rate of interest. Junk bond funds have delivered on that promise during some years, but in other years have fallen far short. In the last quarter of 1989, for example, junk bonds as a group lost 20 percent of their value; in the first quarter of 1990, they fell another 20 percent. That said, there is nothing wrong with having some of your money in a high-yield bond fund, as long as you know what you're buying and have no illusions about its safety.

Three Basic Types of Bond Funds

Bond funds come in many varieties, though not as many as stock funds. The Ratings in chapter 9 classify them according to three broad categories: corporate bond funds, U.S. government and government mortgage funds, and municipal bond funds.

Bear in mind that these categories can be further subdivided according to the average maturities of the bonds the funds hold. The Ratings do that in the case of corporate bond funds, but not for government and municipal bonds, which didn't differ as widely.

The most common divisions are the following:

· Short-term funds usually have an average maturity of less than 3 years.

· Intermediate-term funds usually have an average maturity of 3 to 10 years.

· Long-term funds usually have an average maturity of 10 years or longer.

Average maturity is important because bonds are always at the mercy of changes in interest rates, a danger you may see referred to as "interest rate risk." Simply put, when interest rates on newly issued bonds rise, the value of existing bonds will fall. That stands to reason, since no smart investor would pay the same price for an old bond returning, say, 5 percent interest when new ones are available that will return 6 percent. Conversely, when interest rates on newly issued bonds fall, existing bonds become more valuable.

Because owners of long-term bonds are locked in for a greater period of time and are therefore subject to more months of interest rate risk, long-term bonds and long-term bond funds tend to compensate them with slightly higher rates of interest than their intermediate-term or short-term counterparts. Long-term bond funds can also lose more money when interest rate trends turn against them.

Corporate Bond Funds

For: Investors looking for monthly income and willing to accept slightly greater risks than government bonds entail—in return for slightly greater potential returns.

Not for: Investors hoping to make a great deal of money over the long term and willing to accept the attendant risks. Such investors should probably put the bulk of their money into stock funds, although some money in bond funds can help insulate them from a prolonged stock market decline.

How they work: A corporation issues bonds (and other securities, such as notes and debentures) when it needs to borrow money. Its objective may be to build a new plant or to buy more equipment. It may want to acquire another company or wish to fend off a hostile takeover by making itself unattractively debt-laden. Or its motivations may be tax-related.

Whatever the company's motives, the safety of its bonds will be rated by several bond-rating services. Table 2.1, for example, translates the ratings issued by Standard & Poor's, one of the major rating agencies. Those ratings will help determine the rate of interest that the issuer will have to pay investors who buy its bonds. Issuers whose bonds are perceived as more risky will have to pay more interest.

Corporate bond funds may own hundreds of different bond issues.

TABLE 2.1 HOW BONDS ARE GRADED

These are the ratings used by Standard & Poor's, one of the major bond rating services. Other rating services use their own designations.

AAA is the highest rating. It means the issuers of the bonds have the greatest ability to pay interest and to repay principal in the judgment of the rating service.

AA indicates the next highest ability to meet obligations to bondholders.

A is for bonds from companies that have good credit ratings but that could be affected by economic downturns.

BBB indicates only an adequate capacity to meet obligations. Adverse economic conditions could lead to default.

BB means a speculative bond with substantially more risk.

B means a bond that is among the most risky junk bonds.

B− means a speculative junk bond or possibly a bond that is infrequently traded.

CCC, ratings refer to bonds that are in, or about to go into, default.
CC,
C, D

The quality of their bond portfolios is determined by averaging the ratings of the various issues, taking into account how much money the fund has invested in each class of bond. Our Ratings in chapter 9 do that in a column headed "Quality," using the same AAA to D designations in Table 2.1. Note, however, that bond-fund portfolios are in a constant state of flux, so some funds' average quality may have changed since we looked at them.

A bond fund with mostly high-rated bonds may refer to its portfolio as "investment grade." A fund with mostly low-rated bonds (commonly called junk bonds) may use the term "high-yield."

Corporate bond funds also differ in the average term, or maturity, of the bonds they own. As mentioned, a short-term corporate fund may invest in bonds due to mature in under 3 years. An intermediate-term fund might extend its range out to 10 years. A long-term fund would own bonds with maturities of 10 years and longer. As a general rule, the longer the term, the greater the potential return and the greater the potential risk.

A final factor to examine is a fund's expense ratio. Because bond funds with similar goals will invest in many of the same things, the difference in return between any two funds may be largely a matter of their management fees and operating expenses. Those fees, which shareholders pay, are shown as a percentage of average net assets in each fund's prospectus, under Annual Fund Operating Expenses. They are also reflected in the fund's annual returns, since they are quietly subtracted from its share price.

Most corporate bond funds we rated in 1993 had an annual expense ratio of under 1 percent; some admirably frugal funds managed on a small fraction of that. We'd think twice before buying a bond fund with an expense ratio greater than 1 percent. Nor do we see any reason to pay a load to buy a bond fund, since equally good no-load funds are widely available.

The following corporate bond funds (listed alphabetically and divided into short-, intermediate-, and long-term categories) were top performers in *Consumer Reports'* 1993 Ratings of bond funds. An asterisk (*) indicates the fund doesn't charge a load when you buy or sell shares. Average annual returns are for the years 1988 through 1992.

SHORT-TERM	AVERAGE ANNUAL RETURN
*Scudder Short-Term Bond	9.8%
*Strong Short-Term Bond	9.1
*Vanguard Short-Term Corporate	9.6
INTERMEDIATE-TERM	
*Columbia Fixed-Income Securities	11.0%
Prime Altura Income Bond	9.8
*Vanguard Bond Market	10.4
LONG-TERM	
*Fidelity Investment Grade Bond	10.8%
*Invesco Select Income (formerly Financial Bond Select Income)	10.4
*Vanguard Investment Grade Corporate	12.2

Government Bond Funds

For: Investors who want monthly income and are willing to accept slightly lower returns than corporate bond funds may pay (before taxes are taken into account), in return for the added safety of government securities.

Bear in mind that as much as some government funds like to tout a government "guarantee" of safety, the funds themselves are no more guaranteed than any other type of fund. The guarantee only means that some of the securities in their portfolios, such as Treasury bonds, are backed by the "full faith and credit" of the U.S. government. However, even those securities are guaranteed only with regard to the repayment of their principal; there is no guarantee that they won't lose value if interest rates on newly issued bonds rise.

Not for: As with corporate bond funds, government bond funds should not represent the bulk of a long-term investor's portfolio, since they are unlikely to do as well over time as stock funds. But they can be useful as a counterbalance to riskier investments in a portfolio of several funds.

How they work: The U.S. government and its agencies borrow money by issuing securities. Do they ever. At this writing, the national debt has surpassed $4 trillion, and it's still growing. Much of the money the government borrows today simply goes to pay the interest on the securities it issued earlier.

The U.S. Treasury issues three basic types of securities: bills, notes, and bonds. The major difference is the length of time until they mature.

- Bills are short-term obligations that mature in 1 year or less.
- Notes are medium-term obligations that mature in 1 to 10 years.
- Bonds are long-term obligations that mature in 10 years or longer.

Two advantages of investing in Treasury securities through a mutual fund rather than directly are (1) the funds tend to have lower minimum initial investments, and (2) you can add small amounts of money to your fund at any time. By contrast, to buy Treasury bills directly, you would have to invest at least $10,000. Treasury bonds and some Treasury notes have minimums as low as $1,000, but you would need another $1,000 each time you wanted to add to your holdings. (For more information on buying Treasury securities directly, contact the nearest Federal Reserve Bank or branch.)

The Treasury Department also issues the familiar U.S. Savings Bonds for small investors in denominations ranging from $50 to $10,000, which can be purchased at most banks.

Government bond funds may also invest in securities issued by agencies other than the U.S. Treasury. For example, they may own securities backed by federally insured mortgages or student loans.

Income from funds that invest exclusively in Treasury securities is not subject to state income tax in most states. It is, however, subject to federal income tax, just like income from corporate bond funds.

Like corporate bond funds, government bond funds are subject to risks involving changes in interest rates. A fund whose portfolio has an average maturity of, say, 10 years is considered less risky than one with an average maturity of 25 years. For that reason, the latter fund should pay a higher rate of return.

Also in common with corporate funds, government funds have operating expenses, which are shown in their prospectuses and reflected in their share prices. Since most government funds invest in similar securities, the difference between a good performer and a poor one is often simply a matter of the expenses they impose. Expense ratios greater than 1 percent are high for a government bond fund, in our view.

Finally, many government bond funds have loads, or sales charges, in the 4.0 to 4.75 percent range—with some even higher. We see no reason to sacrifice 4 percent of your money up front to buy an investment that may return little more than that in its first year. Buy a good no-load fund instead.

The following government funds (listed alphabetically) were top performers in *Consumer Reports'* 1993 Ratings of bond funds. An asterisk (*) indicates the fund doesn't charge a load when you buy or sell shares. Average annual returns are for the years 1988 through 1992.

	AVERAGE ANNUAL RETURN
*Fidelity Government Securities	10.4%
Government Income Securities	9.4
*Vanguard Short-Term Federal Portfolio	8.9

3. TAX-FREE MUNICIPAL BOND FUNDS

For: Investors in a sufficiently high tax bracket, for whom these funds' comparatively modest yields will be made up for by their tax advantages.

Not for: Investors for whom tax considerations aren't a significant matter. Tax-free funds are also inappropriate investments for tax-deferred retirement accounts, such as IRAs.

How they work: State and local governments and some of their agencies periodically issue securities that are collectively known as municipal bonds. The money they raise is used to build schools, roads, and hospitals and to finance other public projects.

Aside from the useful works they pay for, municipal bonds appeal to investors because the interest they return is generally not subject to federal income tax. If you live in the state where the bonds were issued, they may also be free from state and local taxes.

Mutual funds that invest in municipal bonds come in several varieties. Some invest in a portfolio of municipal bonds from across the United States. The income from those funds is usually free from federal income tax, but not from state and local income taxes. (This is the type of municipal bond fund shown in the Ratings in chapter 9.)

Other funds invest only in the municipal bonds of a certain state. Single-state funds, as they're often called, earn income that usually isn't subject to federal, state, or local income taxes. For that reason, you may see them advertised as "triple tax-free."

In theory, municipal bond funds that invest in a variety of states should be less risky than those that concentrate on a single state, because they're more diversified. In choosing between the two types of funds, you'll have to balance the lower risk of national funds against the lower taxes you will pay on interest from single-state funds.

Single-state funds make more sense for investors in states with high income-tax rates than they do for investors in low-tax (or no-tax) states. For the latter group, a fund that buys municipal bonds across the United States will usually be a better choice. National municipal bond funds also tend to have lower expense ratios than their single-state counterparts. That is another plus in their favor for investors in all but the most heavily taxed states.

Municipal bonds tend to pay a lower rate of interest than taxable bonds because of their tax advantages. Table 2.2 shows how tax-free yields compare to taxable yields for people in certain tax brackets. Obviously, the higher your bracket, the more alluring those yields may be.

Some money-market funds invest in very short-term municipal bonds. They allow you to write checks against your balance, much like a checking account.

Though not having to pay taxes on your investment earnings may be an enticing prospect, there are a couple of negative aspects to municipal bond funds. First, not all of the income you receive from the fund may be tax-free. If the fund makes a capital-gains distribution, in addition to its regular dividend payments, those capital gains are taxable, just as they would be had they come from a taxable variety of fund. Bond funds make capital-gains distributions when they sell bonds that have appreciated.

Further, municipal bond funds are not appropriate investments for tax-deferred retirement accounts, such as IRAs. The money you accumulate in such an account is considered taxable income when you withdraw it, regardless of what it was invested in. And in an IRA, income is tax-deferred anyway, eliminating any tax advantage a municipal bond fund might otherwise offer. For those reasons, you'd do better to put your IRA money in a higher-yielding, though taxable, investment.

Note of caution to retired investors: Although municipal bond interest is generally tax-free, it must be included in your total income in figuring whether part of your Social Security benefits are taxable. If you receive a substantial amount of income from municipal bonds, you may be better off moving that money into higher-yielding taxable bonds. Those rules are explained in IRS Publication 915, "Social Security Benefits and Equivalent Railroad Retirement Benefits," available from the IRS at 800-TAX-FORM.

The following municipal bond funds (listed alphabetically) were top performers in *Consumer Reports'* 1993 Ratings of bond funds. An asterisk (*) indicates the fund doesn't charge a load when you buy or sell shares. Average annual returns are for the years 1988 through 1992.

	AVERAGE ANNUAL RETURN
*Fidelity High-Yield Tax-Free	10.1%
*USAA Tax Exempt Long-Term	10.1
*Vanguard Municipal Bond High Yield	11.0

TABLE 2.2 HOW TAX-FREE YIELDS COMPARE

To compare the returns on taxable bond funds and tax-free municipal bond funds, you need to consider your income-tax bracket. This chart shows equivalent tax-free and taxable yields for people in five federal income-tax brackets.

A TAX-FREE YIELD OF:	FOR A TAX BRACKET OF:				
	15%	28%	31%	36%	39.6%
	EQUALS A TAXABLE YIELD OF:				
3%	3.5%	4.2%	4.3%	4.7%	5.0%
4	4.7	5.6	5.8	6.2	6.6
5	5.9	6.9	7.2	7.8	8.3
6	7.1	8.3	8.7	9.3	9.9
7	8.2	9.7	10.1	10.9	11.6
8	9.4	11.1	11.6	12.5	13.2
9	10.6	12.5	13.0	14.0	14.9
10	11.8	13.9	14.5	15.6	16.6

For other tax-free yields and other tax brackets, you can use this formula: the tax-free yield divided by (1 minus your tax bracket) equals the equivalent taxable yield. From the table above, for example, 6 divided by (1 minus 0.28) equals 8.3 percent.

4. INDEX FUNDS

For: Investors willing to forgo the services of an active fund manager, knowing that few managers are likely to do better than the indexes year after year, anyway.

Not for: Whether an index fund is an appropriate investment for you will depend on what the fund itself invests in. For example, stock index funds probably aren't appropriate for people who are uncomfortable investing in stocks in the first place. The same would be true for a bond index fund and people for whom bonds are not an appropriate investment. (Those considerations were discussed earlier under both stock and bond funds.)

How they work: Index funds are a relatively recent addition to the fund spectrum. Many of them are just a few years old.

Index funds invest in the securities that make up a particular stock or bond index. An index is a representative sample of the securities that make up a particular market. A number of index funds, for example, track the widely quoted S&P 500 stock market index. Others track one of several small-company stock indexes. Still others track indexes of bonds, gold stocks, gas stocks, various foreign stock markets, and so on.

The case for index funds is simple. Few fund managers beat the indexes in a typical year—and fewer still beat them year after year. So a fund that simply invests in the same holdings as the index is likely to perform better than most other types of funds over time. Index funds also tend to have lower operating expenses than more actively managed funds. For example, the Vanguard Index Trust 500 Portfolio, which invests in the stocks that make up the S&P 500 stock market index, showed management expenses of just 0.20 percent in our 1993 Ratings of mutual funds. That was not only the lowest expense ratio in the growth-and-income category, but half the expense ratio of the next thriftiest fund. Several funds reported expense ratios greater than 2 percent—more than 10 times that of the Vanguard index fund.

Don't automatically assume that just because a fund calls itself an index fund, it necessarily has low expenses. A few index funds manage to rack up expense ratios more in keeping with actively managed funds. So take a hard look at expenses in comparing index funds; you'll find them listed in each fund's prospectus.

The performance of index funds generally lags behind that of the index they mimic because the indexes themselves are simply statistical models with no operating expenses at all. To illustrate that, suppose you had made a series of $2,000 annual investments from 1988 through 1992 in the Vanguard index fund mentioned earlier. By the end of 1992, your account would have been worth $15,333. Had you been able to make those same investments directly in the S&P 500 index, your account would have been worth $15,440, or $107 more. That difference represents the costs of running the fund.

At tax time index funds have an additional advantage over actively managed funds. The more buying and selling of securities a fund does, the more likely it is to have capital gains. By law, the fund must pass those gains on to investors in the form of capital-gains distributions, and the investor must pay income tax on them, unless the fund is part of a tax-deferred account. Because index funds essentially buy and hold whatever stocks or other securities that make up their index, they have little capital gains to report. So given the choice between an index fund and an actively managed fund that turns in a similar performance, you'll be better off, after taxes, with the index fund. You would, of course, have to pay capital-gains taxes when you eventually sold your index-fund shares, assuming they're worth more than you originally paid for them.

One argument against index funds is that they are likely to suffer more than actively managed funds during sustained market declines. An index fund's fortunes are anchored to those of the market it follows; if the market sinks, the fund will be dragged down with it. An actively managed fund, on the other hand, can move in and out of markets as its manager sees fit. A prescient manager might sell stocks before a decline and not lose as much money. Few index funds have been around long enough to test this argument, but it makes sense. If nothing else, it's all the more reason to choose actively managed funds (if you'd prefer them to index funds) whose managers have demonstrated skill in both good economic times and bad.

The Ratings in chapter 9 don't break out index funds separately because few of them had five-year track records at the time of our study. Some index funds that have been in existence for at least five years do appear in the Ratings; you'll find several stock index funds, for example, listed under Growth-and-Income.

Among no-load index funds that invest in the S&P 500 are the

Dreyfus Peoples Index Fund, based in New York City; the Fidelity Market Index Fund, based in Boston; and the Vanguard Index Trust 500 Portfolio, based in Valley Forge, Pennsylvania.

Smaller stocks are represented in the Vanguard Small Capitalization Stock Fund, also based in Valley Forge, Pennsylvania, which tracks the Russell 2000.

Vanguard's Bond Market Fund tracks the Salomon Brothers broad investment-grade bond index.

5. MORTGAGE-BACKED FUNDS

For: People looking for regular income and willing to take a somewhat greater risk than a bond fund might entail, in return for the potential of somewhat higher returns.

Not for: Income investors who can't afford to accept some risk to their capital.

How they work: Mortgage-backed funds invest primarily in securities issued by the Government National Mortgage Association, a corporation set up by the U.S. government. Those securities go by their initials, GNMAs, or the nickname Ginnie Mae. Ginnie Maes represent pools of mortgages that the association has purchased from lenders for resale to investors.

Ginnie Mae securities are backed by the U.S. government, so there is little risk that they will default or fail to make timely interest payments. Other types of mortgage securities may also carry the guarantees of a government agency or a private group.

Reassuring as the guarantees may be, none of them protects investors from what is known as prepayment risk. Prepayment risk is unique to mortgage-backed securities. It works like this: When interest rates drop significantly (say 3 or 4 percentage points), many homeowners will refinance their mortgages at the lower rate. So, for example, a 30-year mortgage at 10 percent may suddenly be paid off by the borrower, only a few years into the loan. The Ginnie Mae fund will have to reinvest that money in new mortgages, which may be paying only 7 or 8 percent.

To compensate investors for prepayment risk, Ginnie Maes and the funds that invest in them typically pay interest rates that are a percentage point or so higher than those on government bonds funds. Such rates may be enticing, particularly when rates are generally low and you're scrambling for somewhere to put your money. But don't count on that rate going on forever.

Note also that Ginnie Mae funds lack the tax advantages of government funds that invest in U.S. Treasury securities. Because the mortgages aren't direct obligations of the U.S. government, the interest they pay is subject to state and local income taxes, as well as to federal tax.

A relatively new type of mortgage fund invests in adjustable-rate mortgages, or ARMs. ARMs, in essence, shift the risk of rising interest rates onto the homeowner rather than the lender. If rates go up, the homeowner must pay more interest. ARMs are subject to very little prepayment risk; there's no strong incentive for homeowners with ARMs to refinance when interest rates drop, since the rate on their mortgages will presumably drop too.

ARM funds haven't been around long enough for us to pass judgment on them. So far, they have trailed conventional Ginnie Mae funds but have also been less volatile—pretty much as one would expect.

The following mortgage-backed funds (listed alphabetically) were top performers in *Consumer Reports'* 1993 Ratings of bond funds. An asterisk (*) indicates the fund doesn't charge a load when you buy or sell shares. Average annual returns are for the years 1988 through 1992.

	AVERAGE ANNUAL RETURN
*Benham GNMA Income	11.0%
*Fidelity Ginnie Mae	10.4
*Vanguard Fixed Income GNMA	11.4

6. REAL ESTATE FUNDS

For: Investors who want to diversify their fund portfolios beyond basic stock and bond funds.

Not for: Investors who would suffer unduly if a long-term commercial real estate slump caused their fund to lose value.

How they work: Mutual funds that invest in real estate are a fairly recent option and still fairly rare. The oldest of them dates back only to 1986.

For the most part, these funds invest in real estate investment trusts, or REITs. REITs, in turn, invest primarily in commercial real estate and mortgages. Real estate mutual funds may also invest in the stocks of companies involved in construction or that have large land holdings.

Real estate funds have not been stellar performers, largely because commercial real estate has been in a slump for most of the time they've been around. But they may make sense for some investors. For one thing, they can pay attractive dividends. For another, the stock market and the real estate market aren't always headed in the same direction, so having some money in a real estate fund can help diversify a portfolio of stock funds.

When real estate funds are included in listings of mutual funds, you'll usually find them listed under Growth-and-Income. Two well-known funds that invest in real estate are Fidelity Real Estate Investment Portfolio, based in Boston, and U.S. Real Estate Fund, based in San Antonio. Both funds are no-loads.

7. INTERNATIONAL AND GLOBAL FUNDS

For: Investors looking to diversify their portfolios beyond the borders of the United States—not a bad idea for just about anyone in today's global economy.

Not for: Investors who want risk-free investments, especially for current income. International funds are subject not only to all the usual market risks but also to currency risk.

How they work: The basic distinction between funds that call themselves global and those that call themselves international is that global funds generally can invest in any country on the globe, including the United States. International funds, by contrast, typically invest only outside the United States. To simplify the following discussion a little, we'll lump both together as international funds.

International funds come in two main varieties: bond funds and stock funds.

• **International bond funds** invest in the bonds of foreign companies and governments. You are, in effect, lending money to a foreign company or government in return for its interest payments. That interest may, in some cases, be higher than what you would be able to obtain from a domestic bond fund.

• **International stock funds** invest in the stocks of foreign corporations. You stand to profit from their growth or to suffer from their misfortunes. To put the growing stock markets of the world into some perspective, today U.S. stocks represent only about a third of the world's stock market—down from two-thirds just 20 years ago.

Though some international funds have been around for decades, more specialized ones have arrived on the scene in recent years. For example, you can now buy index funds pegged to foreign stock and bond markets. International bond funds now come in short-, intermediate-, and long-term varieties, much like domestic bond funds.

International stock funds, meanwhile, now include funds that concentrate on smaller companies with rapid growth prospects, as well as funds that concentrate on established companies. Some international funds focus on certain parts of the world, such as Europe or Asia, or on "emerging markets"—which generally means the developing economies of Latin America, Asia, the Middle East, and Africa. Single-country funds, which are usually structured as closed-end funds, focus even more narrowly.

Whether they invest in bonds or in stocks, international funds have a number of things going for them. First, it's still very difficult for investors to buy foreign securities on their own; a mutual fund makes that simple. At the same time, a fund can provide considerable diversification, not only across companies but across countries. The 1993 annual report for the Scudder International Fund, for example, showed that the fund owned the stocks of 136 companies in 26 countries.

Owning shares in an international stock fund can diversify your portfolio in more ways than mere geography. Foreign stock markets and the U.S. market don't go up and down in sync. If the U.S. market is falling, many foreign markets may be rising, and vice versa. So an international fund can offer not only the growth potential inherent in stocks but also a cushion when the U.S. market stumbles.

International funds can also benefit—or suffer—from changes in the currency markets. If the U.S. dollar falls in value relative to foreign currencies, an international fund's share price can rise, even if its underlying portfolio isn't gaining value. In fact, it can rise even if the portfolio is losing value. Conversely, if the dollar rises against foreign currencies, the share price of the fund can fall, no matter how well the securities it owns are doing. That danger is commonly referred to as currency risk.

Some investors received a vivid lesson in currency risk one week during the fall of 1992, when European currencies fell in value relative to the U.S. dollar. Though the major European markets were up as much as 6 percent for the week, mutual funds that invest in Europe lost nearly 4 percent of their value. Even so, many financial advisers recommend keeping at least a portion of a well-diversified fund portfolio in international funds.

Consumer Reports has not rated international or global bond funds. The following international and global stock funds (listed alphabetically) were top performers in our 1993 Ratings of stock funds. An asterisk (*) indicates the fund doesn't charge a load when you buy or sell shares. Average annual returns are for the years 1988 through 1992.

	AVERAGE ANNUAL RETURN
EuroPacific Growth	13%
*Harbor International	16
*Scudder Global	13

Since we haven't rated international or global bond funds, we can't supply a list similar to the one above for them. But here are the names of a few that have been around for a number of years: Fidelity Global Bond, based in Boston; T. Rowe Price International Bond, based in Baltimore; and Scudder International Bond, based in Boston. All three are no-load funds.

8. SECTOR FUNDS

For: Long-term investors who want to place a bet on the fortunes of a particular industry.

Not for: Beginning investors or any investor who may need all of his or her money back in the near term.

How they work: Sector funds invest in the securities of specific industries. Fidelity Investments, the largest of all sector-fund sponsors, offers three dozen such funds (at this writing). Among the sectors those funds cover are air transportation, automotive, biotechnology, chemicals, computers, environmental services, financial services, paper and forest products, and telecommunications.

Sector funds forgo the broad diversification that has long been one of the hallmarks of mutual funds in order to concentrate on a single industry. On a continuum of risk, they might be placed somewhere between a diversified mutual fund and an individual stock, probably closer to the individual stock.

You'll frequently find one or more sector funds topping the charts in magazine ratings of mutual funds, depending on what sector of the economy happened to have done well during that time period. Chances are you'll also find a bunch of them clustered at the bottom of the ratings. Because sector funds can be so speculative, *Consumer Reports* does not include them in its Ratings of mutual funds.

Still, if you have reason to believe that a certain sector might boom in the years ahead, perhaps because your work brings you into frequent contact with that field, a sector fund is one way to invest in your hunch. We would not recommend sector funds for investors who can't afford to lose any of their capital. Nor would we suggest investing in a sector fund before you have built a solid portfolio of more diversified mutual funds.

Utilities funds, which are often classified as sector funds, are something of an exception to this discussion. They invest in the securities of public utilities, such as gas and electric companies and telephone companies. Because utilities companies tend to pay relatively high stock dividends, many conservative investors buy their stocks for income. Funds that invest in utilities are generally not as risky as funds that invest in other sectors of the economy. They also lack the growth potential of other sector funds, since the companies they invest in are subject to greater government regulation.

Gold and precious-metals funds also are frequently labeled as sector funds.

Fund families with a selection of sector funds available include Fidelity Investments, based in Boston; Invesco Funds Group, based in Denver; and the Vanguard Group, based in Valley Forge, Pennsylvania.

The Fidelity sector funds generally impose sales charges; the Invesco and Vanguard funds are no-loads, though the Vanguard funds carry a 1 percent redemption fee.

9. PRECIOUS-METALS FUNDS

For: Investors concerned about high future inflation, who believe that gold and other precious metals would benefit.

Not for: Investors looking for rapid growth of their capital under normal economic conditions.

How they work: Precious-metals funds invest primarily in the stocks of companies that mine for gold, silver, and platinum. The funds may also own some of the actual metals.

Historically, investors have owned gold and other precious metals as a hedge against severe inflation. And, historically, gold and the other metals provided that hedge. Investors have long been advised by financial planners to keep 5 to 10 percent of their money in a gold fund, just in case.

In recent years, gold has lost much of its luster. One reason is that professional investors now have many other vehicles they can use to hedge against inflation, such as futures and options trading. Another is that with the development of world financial markets and new technologies, money has become much more portable. Fleeing rulers who formerly had to smuggle their fortunes out of the country in gold bars now can transfer their wealth faster than you can say "junta." The Persian Gulf War of 1991, exactly the sort of event that would once have sent gold prices soaring, caused barely a blip in the metals market.

So where does that leave gold? According to many economists and investment advisers, gold is just another commodity—though still a costly one.

Yet, for one reason or another, gold may reward its investors now and then. In early 1993, for example, gold stocks shot up in value. But that was the first good news gold investors had heard in a very long time.

Consumer Reports has not rated precious-metals funds. But if the idea of having some money in one appeals to you, here are a few no-loads you might consider: Lexington Goldfund, based in Saddle Brook, New Jersey; Vanguard Specialized Portfolios—Gold and Precious Metals, based in Valley Forge, Pennsylvania; and USAA Gold, based in San Antonio.

Another way to invest a portion of your portfolio in precious metals is to buy shares of an asset-allocation fund, which we'll describe later in this chapter. Such funds may keep a small percentage of their assets in precious metals.

10. "ETHICAL" AND "SOCIALLY RESPONSIBLE" FUNDS

For: Investors who don't want to put their money in companies or governments whose public policies or business practices they can't condone.

Not for: Investors primarily concerned with the financial performance of their investments.

How they work: The quotation marks in the title of this section are not meant to be snide. They are there simply to recognize that not all of us share precisely the same notion of ethics or social responsibility. Nor do all the funds that describe themselves as ethical or socially responsible invest in precisely the same list of companies.

To date, about 25 mutual funds are marketed to appeal to investors' social concerns. Most of them shun companies that profit from tobacco, alcohol, gambling, nuclear power, or military weapons. Many avoid companies that do business in South Africa. Some also look at how companies behave toward their workers, how they treat the environment, and whether they test their products on animals. At least one fund refuses to buy U.S. Treasury securities, on the grounds that the money could be used to support the U.S. military. A well-managed socially responsible fund with a solid long-term record could, of course, make sense for just about any investor.

Some of these funds invest in stocks, or in both stocks and bonds. There are also socially conscious bond funds and money-market funds.

You can get an idea of a fund's philosophy by reading its prospectus, though that description is likely to be general, at best. Here, for example, is how a 1992 prospectus for the Dreyfus Third Century Fund, one of the better-known socially conscious funds, describes its mission:

> The Fund invests principally in common stocks, or securities convertible into common stock, of companies which, in the opinion of the Fund's management, not only meet traditional investment standards, but also show evidence that they conduct their business in a manner that contributes to the enhancement of the quality of life in America. The Fund does not invest in companies operating in South Africa.

You can get a better idea of a fund's investment practices by looking at its most recent semiannual or annual report. Any fund you're thinking of investing in will send you a copy. That report will list all of the fund's holdings as of a certain date. While you can't be expected to know everything about the business practices of every company on that list, you may spot some whose policies you would not endorse.

Pay particular attention to the portfolios of funds that advertise an interest in the environment. Some of them look for companies with pristine environmental records. Others simply invest in companies that stand to make a profit from the environment in one way or another, such as through waste hauling.

If you do decide to invest in one of these funds, don't be so distracted by the "warm glow" it gives you that you ignore its performance record. As a group, socially responsible funds have sometimes outperformed the general market and sometimes lagged behind it. Within the group, returns have varied widely. All ethical considerations being equal, buy the fund with the best long-term record.

Also take a look at the funds' loads, or sales charges. They can siphon off as much as 7.25 percent of your investment, simply to reward the broker who sold you the fund or to profit the company that sponsors it. Surprisingly, for a group of funds that is so critical of other companies' business practices, only a few of these funds are no-loads.

Among companies that offer one or more socially conscious mutual funds are Calvert Group, in Bethesda, Maryland; Dreyfus Corporation, in New York City; New Alternatives Fund, in Great Neck, New York; the Parnassus Fund, in San Francisco; Pax World Fund, in Portsmouth, New Hampshire; and Working Assets, in San Francisco.

11. ASSET-ALLOCATION FUNDS

For: Investors who want a high degree of diversification but who don't want to own a lot of individual funds. An asset-allocation fund may also be a good first fund for a beginning investor without a great deal of money.

Not for: Investors who want to choose separate funds to provide adequate diversification for their portfolios.

How they work: The theory behind asset allocation is simple enough: Different types of assets perform differently at different times. For example, inflation is usually bad news for the stock market, but good news for real estate values. Low interest rates are good for stock prices, but don't do anything for precious metals. So, the theory goes, it should be possible to construct a portfolio that can weather the usual economic storms and reward its investor with superior performance over time.

In search of that perfect portfolio, asset-allocation funds invest in stocks of different types, bonds of different maturities, real estate securities, and precious metals, among other things. Some have fixed portfolios that allocate a certain percentage of their money to a certain type of asset and never vary it, no matter what. Others allow their managers to shift investments around as conditions change.

The record of asset-allocation funds is mixed, and many of them have not been around long enough to experience a significant market downturn. In fact, many of them were launched in the aftermath of the 1987 stock market crash, to appeal to jittery investors.

You can also try your own version of asset allocation by diversifying among a group of different mutual funds. (Chapter 4 explores some strategies and includes a chart showing model asset-allocation plans.)

If the concept of asset-allocation funds appeals to you, also take a look at two similar categories of funds explained elsewhere in this chapter: balanced funds (listed under stock funds) and funds that invest in other funds (see pages 19 and 51).

Funds that practice an asset-allocation strategy include Fidelity Asset Manager and Fidelity Asset Manager—Growth Fund, based in Boston; USAA Cornerstone, based in San Antonio; and Vanguard Asset Allocation, based in Philadelphia. All are no-loads.

12. MONEY-MARKET FUNDS

For: Any investor.

Not for: See above.

How they work: Money-market funds will be only briefly touched on in this book, since they are more a savings tool than an investment vehicle. Still, they can play an important role in your fund investing.

Money-market funds are, in essence, very short-term bond funds. They invest in short-term government securities, commercial paper, and bank certificates-of-deposit. Some specialize in one type of security, such as U.S. Treasury bills; others buy whatever looks good to their managers at the moment.

Still other money-market funds invest in tax-free municipal bonds. The interest those funds pay is not subject to federal income tax and, depending on where you live and where the securities were issued, may not be subject to state or local income taxes, either. Such funds are much like the tax-free municipal bond funds described earlier in this chapter.

A relatively recent phenomenon are money-market funds that invest in foreign securities. Because they may be subject to currency fluctuations and other dangers, they should be considered riskier than the domestic variety.

Unlike other types of mutual funds, domestic money-market funds maintain a stable share price of $1 a share. They pay investors interest, usually monthly. You can take that interest in the form of monthly income or have it automatically reinvested in more shares. Automatic reinvestment is an easy way to build up your fund's balance.

Don't confuse money-market mutual funds with the so-called money-market accounts offered by banks—as much as your bank might like you to confuse the two. Money-market mutual funds pay a substantially higher rate of interest than banks do.

Money-market mutual funds are not federally insured, as most bank accounts are. But they have proven very safe over the years. Some of them invest solely in U.S government securities, which gives them an added layer of safety, though usually at the cost of a somewhat reduced yield.

Most, if not all, major mutual-fund companies offer one or more money-market mutual funds. When you open your account, you will generally receive a packet of checks you can use to withdraw money from your account as needed. That can be a major convenience to you if you need to cash in some of your shares in another fund in that family. All you need do is transfer money from that fund into your money-market fund, then write a check on your money-market account. By the same token, you can use a money-market fund as a place to park money until you decide which funds to transfer it into for the long term.

Keep in mind, though, that most money-market funds specify a minimum amount for the checks you write, such as $250 or $500. You probably don't want to use a money-market fund as your everyday checking account.

In shopping for a money-market mutual fund, consider two additional factors:

Convenience. Is the money-market fund part of a family of funds that's large and diverse enough to meet your needs as an investor? How many checks will you be allowed to write on your account each month? What is the minimum amount you can write a check for?

Performance. Since most money-market funds invest in more or less the same securities, their returns tend not to diverge as widely as returns do for most other types of funds. A key variable is how much money your fund skims off to pay its expenses. Some money-market funds are notoriously tightfisted with expenses; others are far more generous toward themselves. When you call to get a prospectus for a money-market fund, ask about its expense ratio—anything approaching 1 percent should probably be considered high.

Also be sure to ask whether that expense ratio reflects normal conditions or whether the fund is absorbing some of its expenses for a limited period of time. In recent years, some new funds have done that in order to attract early investors. You have no guarantee that the expenses will stay at that low level for long—and no way of knowing how high they'll go once they begin to rise. Our advice: Choose a fund that keeps its expenses low as a matter of principle rather than as a marketing gimmick.

13. CLOSED-END FUNDS

For: It depends, of course, on what the fund invests in, but closed-end funds are usually for relatively experienced investors who are comfortable with a fair amount of risk.

Not for: Beginners.

How they work: Like money-market funds, closed-end funds are beyond the basic scope of this book. *Consumer Reports* has not rated them. But here, in brief, is what they're all about.

Closed-end funds resemble open-end mutual funds in many respects. Some of them, in fact, are offered by the same investment groups as open-end funds and may even be run by the same managers. But the two types of funds differ in several fundamental ways.

First, while open-end funds create new shares whenever investors want to buy them, closed-end funds have only a fixed (or closed) number of shares. After their initial public offering, closed-end funds are traded on stock exchanges or on the over-the-counter market. The common advice is never to buy a closed-end fund at its initial offering, since share prices almost always fall once the fund begins trading on the stock market.

Also unlike open-end funds, closed-end funds may sell for more or less than the value of their holdings, depending on market supply and demand. A fund selling for more than its holdings are worth is said to be selling at a premium; a fund selling for less is said to be selling at a discount.

Like open-end mutual funds, closed-end funds fall into certain broad categories. Some invest primarily in stocks, some in bonds, some in a combination of the two. Others specialize in particular industries or foreign stock markets. Such single-country funds include the Argentina Fund, the Germany Fund, the Irish Investment Fund, the Korea Fund, the Mexico Fund, the Spain Fund, and the Taiwan Fund. You can find those and many others listed in the business pages of most major newspapers, either separately or as part of the listing for the stock exchange they trade on.

In general, closed-end funds are somewhat more difficult to buy, to sell, and to research than open-end funds. They also have to be purchased through a broker, which means paying a brokerage commission—unlike no-load open-end funds, which are commission-free. For all of those reasons, most investors will probably want to stick to open-end funds.

14. FUNDS THAT INVEST IN OTHER FUNDS

For: Investors who want a highly diversified mutual fund, perhaps as their first fund or as their only one.

Not for: Investors who want to build their own diversified portfolio of funds.

How they work: A handful of mutual funds will invest your money in other funds. Their objective is much like that of asset-allocation funds: one-stop diversification. Some of these funds invest in mutual funds offered by their parent company; others invest in funds sold by several companies.

T. Rowe Price's Spectrum Growth Fund, to choose one, invests in seven other T. Rowe Price funds, including aggressive-growth, growth-and-income, and international funds. The company also offers a similarly diversified Spectrum Income Fund.

Funds that invest in other funds are unlikely to outperform a good stock fund over the long term. But they are also likely to be less volatile. As a result, they may appeal to investors who can't afford (financially or psychologically) or simply don't wish to take big risks with their money. They may also be appropriate for investors who are just getting started in fund investing and don't have enough money to buy a diversified portfolio of separate mutual funds.

Some well-known funds that invest in other funds are T. Rowe Price Spectrum Growth and T. Rowe Price Spectrum Income, based in Baltimore, and Vanguard STAR, based in Valley Forge, Pennsylvania. All are no-load funds.

3 WHERE AND HOW TO BUY MUTUAL FUND SHARES

In recent years, investing money in a mutual fund has become easier in most ways, but more difficult in a few others. It's easier because funds are sold in far more places. Several mutual fund companies now have walk-in centers in major cities. Many banks now sell mutual funds. One major airline even has its own line of mutual funds and distributes prospectuses for them to the passengers on its planes.

Fund shopping also is easier now because objective information is widely obtainable. A growing number of independent fund-rating services, financial magazines, and other publications (including *Consumer Reports*) publish unbiased guidance on which funds to buy.

But at the same time, the task of buying fund shares has also become more confusing. For one thing, there are more funds and more types of funds from which to choose every year. Just a decade ago in 1983, there were 1,026 mutual funds available to investors; today there are more than three times that number. In 1983 there was no such thing as an asset-allocation fund; today there are more than a dozen.

More important, the fees that funds impose have become more varied and trickier to evaluate. The world of mutual funds once could be neatly split into the good guys and the bad guys, depending on the fees they charged their investors. The good guys were no-load funds: They imposed no loads, or commissions, when you bought shares. The bad, or at least less good, guys were the load funds: They skimmed off as much as 8.5 percent of every dollar you invested simply to reward the broker or financial planner who talked you into buying that fund.

Today, 8.5 percent load funds are largely history. But other fees have proliferated. Many funds are now "low loads," charging 2 or 3 percent commissions when you invest. Other funds levy a fee for each year you stay in the fund. Others charge a commission when you sell your fund shares. Still others employ a combination of fees that, taken together over time, may ultimately cost the investor as much as the maximum up-front load would have.

The following is a quick guide to your choices of where to buy mutual funds.

WAYS TO PURCHASE MUTUAL FUNDS

Buying Directly from the Fund

In order to take a hands-on role in managing your money and to avoid extra fees, you can select your own funds and buy them directly from the fund company that offers them. (You may even have some fun in the process.) If you do your homework, you probably won't need the advice of a salesperson, such as a broker or financial planner, to choose mutual funds.

Buying Through a Full-Service Broker

To buy stocks or corporate bonds, you generally need the services of a stockbroker. Not so for mutual funds. As mentioned above, it's easy (and for many people, preferable) to buy mutual funds directly from the company that sponsors them.

Nevertheless, mutual funds are becoming an increasingly important part of the brokerage business. In 1992, a year in which the industry's revenues rose by a modest 3.5 percent overall, its revenues from mutual fund sales rose by a staggering 31.2 percent. That translated to $2.8 billion in revenue from mutual fund sales. No wonder, as Table 8.1

(page 123) shows, brokerage firms are well represented among the largest fund families. Such familiar names as Merrill Lynch, Dean Witter, and Smith Barney Shearson now rank among the biggest fund sponsors in terms of assets.

Buying through a broker generally means paying a sales charge of up to 7.25 percent. In that case, for every $100 you give the broker, only $92.75 will be invested on your behalf, and $7.25 will be taken off the top.

What does the sales commission get you? Many brokers will tell you that it buys their expert advice, backed by their brokerage firm's vast research resources. Indeed, advice is about all you're buying, and it may be good advice or terrible advice.

Fund industry statistics are revealing on this point. They show that people who buy funds directly, presumably the most knowledgeable group of fund investors, often choose very different types of funds than do investors who buy their funds from brokers or other salespeople. In 1990, for example, only 15 percent of the money invested in high-yield bond funds (commonly called junk bonds) came from direct investors. A whopping 85 percent of junk bond purchases came through brokers and other salespeople. Junk bond funds finished the year down nearly 11 percent on average, not accounting for any sales loads skimmed off the top. For investors who acted on it, the advice to buy a junk bond fund proved pretty costly.

There are a number of red flags to watch for in dealing with a broker or other sellers of financial products:

· Does the broker understand your goals and fears and recommend investments with them in mind?

· Does the broker explain the risks of every investment and not simply throw around words such as "safe" and "guaranteed"?

· Does the broker present mutual funds as long-term investments, as they are meant to be, rather than as investments to be traded frequently? A broker who tries to persuade you to sell a fund you recently bought and invest in another fund could simply be doing it in order to earn another commission. That practice is known as "churning," and it's a violation of the securities laws.

Perhaps to counter consumer resistance to sales loads and other charges, the ever-resourceful brokerage industry has been pushing a new fee arrangement called a "wrap" account in recent years. Such accounts do away with many individual fees and instead charge investors a flat percentage, typically 3 percent of the money they have in the account, every year. One of the products brokers can sell to a wrap account investor is no-load mutual funds; the 3 percent fee, year after year, more than makes up for the lack of a sales charge. Wrap accounts also tend to require high minimum investments, generally $100,000.

Wrap accounts have not been around long enough to prove themselves a good (or bad) thing for investors. But knowledgeable observers of the brokerage scene are skeptical. The financial newspaper *Barron's* summed them up this way in a December 1992 headline: "A New Type of Brokerage Account is Great—for Brokers."

A broker may also tell you that he or she can sell you funds you cannot buy directly. In some cases, this is true. There are funds that are sold only through brokers and are impossible to buy without paying a commission. There are also lines of mutual funds, called "proprietary" funds, that are sold only by one brokerage firm. However, for any mutual fund that a broker can sell you, there is at least one with similar goals and an equally good performance record available from a no-load fund family.

If you already own load funds that you bought from a broker, but have decided to switch your allegiance to no-loads, don't rush to sell your old load funds. If they are performing well, you may want to hold on to them. You've already paid the sales charge, and there's no getting it back. Chalk it up to your investment education.

(For a more thorough discussion of your rights as a brokerage customer, see *Stand Up to Your Stockbroker,* Consumer Reports Books, 1991.)

Buying from a Discount Broker

Discount brokers are the no-frills version of conventional, full-service stockbrokers. They don't offer investment advice but simply execute the trades you tell them to, usually at a fraction of the cost charged by full-service brokers.

Discount brokers, too, have gotten into the mutual fund act. Discount broker Charles Schwab & Co., for example, offers funds from more than 90 different fund families (at this writing). About 200 of those funds are no-loads available with no transaction fees; Schwab receives its fee from the fund company for bringing in customers.

Buying funds through a discount broker may make sense if you already have stocks and bonds in a brokerage account; at the very least, it may simplify your financial paperwork. It may also make sense if you intend to switch money frequently from fund family to fund family. Such speculative tactics, however, are only for the most sophisticated fund investors, and most investors will do well to think of mutual funds as long-term commitments.

Buying Through a Financial Planner

There are three basic types of financial planners you might hire to help you choose mutual funds.

1. **Fee-only planners** are paid by their clients for the advice they offer. Their charges may be expressed either as a flat fee or as an hourly rate. They may also charge you an annual fee for monitoring your investment portfolio.
2. **Commission-only planners** don't charge their clients for advice but instead receive commissions from the companies whose financial products they sell.
3. **Fee-plus-commission planners** charge clients for advice and also receive commissions on the products they sell.

Fee-only planners obviously have no incentive to steer their clients into particular mutual funds just to earn a commission. Unfortunately, fee-only planners are a tiny minority in the financial-planning business.

Since most financial planners depend on commissions for a living, it's not surprising that they strongly favor load funds. A 1992 survey by the trade magazine *Financial Planning* found that "an impressive 99 percent [of readers] report they have recommended a load fund within the past year . . . 31 percent have recommended a no-load fund."

If there was any good news in that survey, it was that the average load on the funds the magazine's readers had sold in the previous year was 4.1 percent—a figure that for 85 percent of them was lower than the average load of five years before. Part of the reason may be that investors have become better educated about loads and more willing to balk at the prospect of paying the maximum legal load, however persuasive the planner's pitch.

But front-end loads are not the only way financial planners make money or the only incentive they have to steer you toward a particular product. Another lure is called a "trail fee." That's a commission the planner receives each year you keep your money in a fund. A planner might explain that a trail fee is simply the compensation for continuing to monitor an investment; another explanation is that the fee is meant to keep a planner from talking an investor into moving money into another fund, just to earn the planner a fresh sales load. The *Financial Planning* survey reported that 63 percent of its readers were receiving higher trail fees than five years before.

Buying at a Bank

Banks have tried to sell mutual funds to their depositors for well over a decade, but it wasn't until the early 1990s that their sales pitch really caught on.

In 1987 mutual funds sold through banks collectively had $35 billion in assets, according to Lipper Analytical Services. Just five years later, that figure had quadrupled to $150 billion, or 10 percent of all mutual fund assets.

What happened? Low interest rates on conventional bank products such as CDs and money-market accounts had sent savers, many of whom had probably never owned a mutual fund share, scrambling for other places to put their money. Banks that could offer mutual funds as an alternative to their depositors were able to keep much of that money from going out the door.

Some mutual funds sold through banks have had solid performance records, a fact that their sponsors have spent great sums to advertise. But before you decide to do your mutual fund investing at the same place you keep your checking account, there are a couple of cautions to be aware of.

First, most banks charge loads on the funds they sell. In fact, an industry survey found that at the end of 1991, 69 percent of banks that sold mutual funds offered only funds with loads, up from 42 percent just five years earlier.

Most loads on bank mutual funds are in the 4 to 5 percent range, meaning that the bank automatically withdraws $4 or $5 from every $100 you invest. That must have come as a shock to many of the first-time investors drawn to mutual funds by low interest rates; they were accustomed to the bank paying them money, not the other way around.

Banks that sell no-load funds may also impose a transaction charge or other fees. Buying a no-load fund directly from the fund sponsor, as described earlier in this chapter, will be less expensive.

Second, and perhaps more important, investors should also keep in mind that the federal deposit insurance that protects their bank accounts does not extend to mutual funds bought at a bank. Bank mutual funds are no safer than mutual funds bought in any other manner. They may even be less safe, because the Securities and Exchange Commission (SEC), which regulates the mutual fund industry, has less authority over banks' activities.

That said, you may find that the convenience of investing through your bank makes up for the added expense. Some banks, for example, let you buy and sell fund shares through their automatic teller machines; some also apply the balance in your fund accounts toward your total balance to determine whether you're eligible for free checking and other perks. Finally, owning mutual funds that you bought at a bank is probably better for your long-term financial health than owning no mutual funds at all.

If you're determined to buy funds from a bank, don't feel obliged to stay with your current bank. Shop around for the best combination of funds, fees, and services.

UNDERSTANDING THE PROSPECTUS

Whenever and wherever you buy a mutual fund, the SEC requires that the seller give you a prospectus. When you request information on a certain fund directly from a fund company, the packet of materials you receive will typically include a prospectus, an application form, and other sales literature. You should take the time to read the material to help decide whether the fund is right for you.

When you buy a fund from a broker, the broker is allowed to furnish a prospectus later, when you receive confirmation of your fund purchase. In other words, when it's too late to change your mind. Our advice: Insist on a prospectus, and take it home and read it before you agree to buy.

A prospectus is not the most inviting of reading material. The financial writer Andrew Tobias was exaggerating only slightly when he defined a prospectus as "a fat legal document you will not read, filled with warnings, risks, and disclosures you will ignore."

But a prospectus does contain some essential information that can guide you in deciding whether to buy a particular fund. It can also be of great help in choosing among similar funds, since the information in a prospectus is presented in a standard, SEC-mandated format to allow for comparison.

Here are five key things to look for.

1. The fund's investment objective. This section will explain the fund's basic goal. The prospectus will also explain the fund's investment policies—that is, the types of securities it invests in and the investment techniques it practices in pursuit of its goal. Many times, the fund's objective will already be clear from the fund's name.

This is the objective of the Fidelity Magellan Fund, as expressed in a 1993 prospectus: "**Goal:** capital appreciation (increase in the value of the fund's shares). As with any mutual fund, there is no assurance that the fund will achieve its goal."

The prospectus continues, "**Strategy:** to invest primarily in common stock, and securities convertible into common stock, of U.S., multinational, and foreign companies of all sizes that offer potential for growth."

The prospectus continues from there, further elaborating on how the fund operates. But you could probably tell by this point whether the fund's objective is consistent with your own. If, for example, you were shopping for a fund that would pay you regular dividend income, this fund obviously would not be an appropriate choice.

2. Fees and operating expenses. Much of the information you'll need to evaluate the various types of fees you may have to pay is included in the prospectus, often in a fairly standard, tablelike format, usually on page 2. Returning to the Fidelity Magellan Fund prospectus, see the following page for a presentation of some of the things it would tell you on the subject of expenses.

From the first list of expenses, you can see that the fund would charge you a load of 3 percent if you bought shares, but it wouldn't

EXPENSES

Shareholder transaction expenses are charges you pay when you buy or sell shares of a fund.

Maximum sales charge on purchases (as a % of offering price)	3.00%
Maximum sales charge on reinvested dividends	None
Deferred sales charge on redemptions	None
Exchange fee	None

Annual fund operating expenses are paid out of the fund's assets. The fund pays management fees to FMR that vary based on the fund's performance. It also incurs other expenses for services such as maintaining shareholder records and furnishing shareholder statements and fund reports. The fund's expenses are factored into its share price or dividends and are not charged directly to shareholder accounts.

The following are projections based on historical expenses, and are calculated as a percentage of average net assets.

Management fee	.75%
12b-1 fee	None
Other expenses	.25%
Total fund operating expenses	1.00%

Source: Fidelity Investments

charge an additional load if you later sold them. From the second list, you can see that the fund's annual operating expenses come to 1.00 percent of the assets in the fund. That means that for every $1,000 you invest, the fund would take out $10 each year to cover its costs.

In the adjoining table, the prospectus also shows what you would pay in expenses on a $1,000 investment over a 1-, 3-, 5-, or 10-year period, assuming that the fund returned 5 percent each year and that you sold your shares at the end of each time period. In the case of this fund, the prospectus shows that expenses would be $40 after 1 year, $61 after 3 years, $84 after 5 years, and $149 after 10 years. The 5 percent return that the table assumes is mandated by the SEC for comparison purposes and has nothing to do with what the fund will actually return in future years.

These numbers may all seem fairly abstract by themselves, but they can be very useful in comparing funds with similar objectives and similar performance results. All other things being equal, you'll be best served by the fund that keeps its fees and operating expenses to a minimum.

3. Financial history. This table represents a capsule history of the fund's performance, expressed in terms of a single share. The example on pages 62–63 is from the same Fidelity Magellan Fund prospectus. In addition to the information on expenses, a key number to look at here is the portfolio turnover rate, listed in this prospectus under the heading "Ratios." Turnover refers to the percentage of the fund's portfolio that was sold and replaced with other securities during the year. That can be a useful gauge of how aggressive a fund is in its pursuit of profits.

Because buying and selling securities involves brokerage costs, a fund with less turnover will generally have lower operating expenses. But it's fair to compare the turnover rates only on funds with similar objectives. An aggressive fund like Fidelity Magellan will, by its very nature, have more turnover than its less-aggressive counterparts.

4. How to buy shares. This section tells you the minimum initial investment the fund will accept, as well as the minimum for additional investments. It will also give you information on buying shares by mail, switching your money over from another fund, or having your bank electronically transfer money.

5. How to sell shares. This section explains how you can redeem your shares when the time comes. Though that day may seem far off, making yourself familiar with the procedures for selling could save you some frustration later on.

Those are five areas of the prospectus that are worth taking a few minutes to explore. The prospectus has other information on the fund that you may want to at least skim. Don't be intimidated—you'll become more comfortable with prospectuses as you gain more experience as a fund investor.

For even more detailed information about the fund and its policies, request a document called a Statement of Additional Information free of charge from the fund company. Also known as Part B of the prospectus, it will tell you what securities the fund owned at the end of its last fiscal year and who the fund's directors and officers are.

As a small experiment, *Consumer Reports* called the toll-free phone numbers of a dozen different fund companies across the United States

FINANCIAL HISTORY

This information has been audited by Coopers & Lybrand, independent accountants. Their unqualified report is included in the fund's Annual Report. The Annual Report is incorporated by reference into (is legally a part of) the Statement of Additional Information.

Per-Share Data

Fiscal years ended March 31	1984	1985	1986	1987	1988	1989	1990	1991	1992	1993
Investment income	$.63	$1.11	$.76	$.81	$1.17	$1.64	$1.90	$1.98	$1.35	$1.77
Expenses	.26	.32	.27	.39	.54	.55	.55	.59	.54	.57
Net investment income	.37	.79	.49	.42	.63	1.09	1.35	1.39	.81	1.20
Distributions from net investment income	(.26)	(.37)	(.65)	(.46)	(.72)	(.90)	(1.24)	(.83)	(1.30)	(1.25)
Net realized & unrealized gain (loss) on investments	2.73	5.75	19.59	11.39	(6.64)	8.63	9.39	8.10	9.21	9.18
Distributions from net realized gain on investments	(1.88)	(3.69)	(1.78)	(6.84)	(9.02)	—	(3.82)	(2.42)	(5.43)	(8.82)
Net increase (decrease) in net asset value	.96	2.48	17.65	4.51	(15.75)	8.82	5.68	6.24	3.29	.31

Net asset value (NAV) beginning of year	34.25	35.21	37.69	55.34	59.85	44.10	52.92	58.60	64.84	68.13
Net asset value at end of year	$35.21	$37.69	$55.34	$59.85	$44.10	$52.92	$58.60	$64.84	$68.13	$68.44

Ratios

Ratio of net investment income to average net assets	1.47%	2.79%	1.95%	1.18%	1.33%	2.13%	2.54%	2.47%	1.57%	2.11%
Ratio of expenses to average net assets	1.04%	1.12%	1.08%	1.08%	1.14%	1.08%	1.03%	1.06%	1.05%	1.00%
Ratio of management fee to average net assets	.67%	.83%	.82%	.77%	.79%	.80%	.73%	.78%	.78%	.75%
Portfolio turnover rate*	85%	126%	96%	96%	101%	87%	82%	135%	172%	155%
Shares outstanding at end of year (in thousands)	45,757	62,716	109,975	165,230	191,353	181,912	224,610	228,377	290,995	363,632

*In accordance with a Securities and Exchange Commission rules amendment, portfolio turnover rates after 1984 include U.S. government long-term securities that were excluded from the calculations in prior years.

Source: Fidelity Investments

to request prospectuses and application forms. On average, we found, the materials reached us in three to five business days. When we requested prospectuses and applications by mail, we had to wait one to three additional days, presumably to allow for our letter to reach the fund company. If you need fund materials faster than that, such as to meet an IRA deadline, call the fund's toll-free number and ask if it has a nearby walk-in center where you can pick up a prospectus.

BUYING FUND SHARES

Buying shares of a mutual fund is no more difficult than filling out a brief application and returning it to the fund. The application will ask whether the account should be set up for an individual or as a joint account for two people. You may also have the option of setting it up as a trust or as a gift or transfer to a minor.

The application will ask how much you want to invest initially. Most funds today have minimum initial investments of $1,000 to $3,500 for non-IRA accounts and lower minimums for IRAs. You will also have to decide whether you want any dividends or capital gains paid to you by check or reinvested in the fund to buy more shares. If you don't need that money for current income, having it reinvested is an easy way to build your fund holdings. Beware, though, of funds that charge loads on reinvested dividends—an unjustifiable nickeling-and-diming of investors, in our view. Also note that for tax purposes, any dividends or capital gains earned (except in a tax-deferred account) will be considered income, regardless of whether you receive them as a check or as additional shares.

The application form will also ask if you are interested in any special services the fund company offers, such as transferring money to or from your bank account via a phone call. Many fund services can be genuine conveniences, but if you don't sign up for them when you first apply, don't worry. They can usually be added later by contacting the fund and changing your instructions.

After the application and a check to the fund of your choice is received, you will be sent a confirmation statement. It will show how much money was invested and how many shares you now own. The number of shares will be expressed out to three decimal places. For example, if you invest $1,000 in a fund that costs $17.07 a share, you will find you now own 58.582 shares. The price paid for each share will depend on the fund's share price at the close of trading on the day the fund received your money. You can check its accuracy in the appropriate issue of a daily newspaper or the *Wall Street Journal.*

If the fund purchased charges a load, that money will be subtracted from your investment before the fund calculates how many shares you own. The price you must pay for a share of a load fund is called the "buy" price or "offer" price in most newspaper listings of mutual funds. A second price column in most newspaper listings is called "net asset value" or simply NAV. It represents what you would get for a share if you wanted to sell it. For a load fund, the NAV will be lower than the buy price on any given day. For no-load funds that impose 12b-1 fees, the two price columns will report the same number; for pure no-loads without 12b-1 fees, one column will show NL for no-load.

UNDERSTANDING THE FEES THAT FUNDS CHARGE

Mutual fund companies have been so resourceful in inventing new fees in the past decade that you may well come across fees that weren't even in existence when this book was written. Nevertheless, here's a list of the fees we've seen so far. They're listed roughly in terms of how much they can cost you, beginning with the costliest fees.

Front-end Loads

Many funds impose a sales charge, or load, as soon as they have your money. Usually loads are expressed as a percentage of your investment. By law, loads may go as high as 8.5 percent, though load funds of 4 to 5 percent appear to be more common these days. Some funds, called low-loads, charge loads of 1 to 3 percent.

The sales pitch you're likely to hear for load funds is that the load compensates the person who sold you the fund for his or her expert advice. Believe that if you wish, although as we explained earlier in this chapter, there's reason to be skeptical.

Don't, however, fall for the old line that load funds perform better than no-loads. Any number of studies have shown that to be nonsense. When *Consumer Reports* looked at the performance of more than 1,000 stock funds over the five-year period 1988 to 1992, we found that the no-load funds had an average annual return of 13.5 percent, compared with a slightly lower 13.3 percent for the load funds. Those figures, incidentally, didn't account for the loads that the load funds charge. Had loads been included in our calculations, the load funds would have fared considerably worse by comparison.

Of course, there's no logical reason why a load would improve performance. After all, the load simply goes to reward the salesperson. The person responsible for performance, the fund's manager, never sees a cent of it.

Back-end Loads

Some funds impose loads when you sell shares. One variety, called a contingent deferred sales charge, declines over time. For example, you might have to pay 5 percent of the value of your shares if you sell them within a year of buying them. In the second year, the charge might be 4 percent, and so on until the charge disappears altogether. Some funds also impose redemption fees or exit fees, typically of 1 or 2 percent, when shares are sold. Any of these fees may seem innocent enough when you buy a fund, but they can be quite costly if a financial emergency forces you to sell earlier than you'd expected to.

12b-1 Fees

Named after the section of the federal law that authorized them, 12b-1 fees force investors to pay some of the fund's advertising and sales expenses. Before the SEC changed the rules in 1993, 12b-1 fees couldn't exceed 1.25 percent a year. Today the maximum is 0.75, plus another 0.25 percent that's allowed as a "service fee." But even 0.75 percent a year, year after year, can add up to a substantial chunk of money—*your* money.

As front-end loads have declined in recent years (probably caused by the increasing sophistication of fund consumers), 12b-1 fees have become more common. Some funds use them to compensate salespeople who earlier would have made their money from the front-end load. By eliminating front-end loads, such funds appear more like no-load funds—and become easier to sell to consumers who mistakenly think they're buying an authentic no-load.

Some fund experts refer to 12b-1 fees as "hidden loads." But fortunately, funds can't hide them entirely. They must be listed in the fund's prospectus, in the table that shows its annual expenses. This is another reason to obtain a prospectus before you invest. All else being equal, go with a fund that charges no 12b-1 fee.

Annual Operating Expenses

No fund is 100 percent fee-free. All fund companies charge investors for managing the fund and for related expenses such as legal and accounting fees. Those expenses are commonly expressed in a percentage called the "expense ratio." You can determine a fund's expense ratio by dividing its expenses by its average net assets. Included in the expense ratio is the fund's 12b-1 fee, if any. As a general rule, bond funds have lower expense ratios than stock funds, since they are less costly to manage. An average bond fund might have an expense ratio of 1.0 percent; an average stock fund, 1.5 percent. Index funds, which simply buy the stocks that make up a particular market index, have lower expense ratios than funds whose managers trade actively. We recommend taking a hard look at any stock fund whose expense ratio is higher than 1.5 percent to see whether there's some justification for its high expenses.

Note that some funds will waive certain fees or absorb part of their operating expenses, especially when they first come on the market. Usually, they will promise to keep that fee structure for a certain period of time, but after that period comes to an end, you may find yourself socked with hefty fees. Funds that keep their fees to a minimum all along, and not just as a promotional stunt, are a better bet. So beware of any funds that indicate their current fee structure will be in effect for only a limited period of time.

Note also that some fund companies sell several "classes" of the same mutual fund, with different sets of fees. (You'll see a number of such funds in the Ratings in chapter 9; they're the ones with a capital A or B at the end of their names.) Class A shares, for example, may charge front-end loads. Class B shares may charge no load up front but instead hit you with a back-end load when you sell, plus a 12b-1 fee each year. Some fund companies also have class C and class D shares—with other variations and letters of the alphabet surely to follow. Though fund salespeople may tell you that the different classes give consumers a choice of when and how to pay sales charges, we don't see that as much of a plus. Unless you really need the salesperson's advice in choosing funds, avoid all these extra fees by buying true no-load funds.

The most important thing to remember about fees is this: It isn't any single fee, but all the fees a fund charges in combination, that will affect your return. Table 3.1 shows the impact of some common combinations of fees on an investment of $2,000 over five time periods. We assumed a 5 percent return, as the SEC requires funds to do in calculating the impact of their fees. Obviously, your return on a fund could be considerably higher than 5 percent—or considerably lower.

INVESTING ON A REGULAR BASIS

Once you have made an initial investment in a mutual fund, you may want to add more money to your account periodically. Putting money

---

TABLE **3.1** **HOW FEES CAN CUT YOUR RETURNS**

In a contest between mutual funds performing equally well, funds with a front-end load but low annual expenses can eventually overtake no-load funds with high annual costs. But, as the examples here show, the combination of no load and low costs is unbeatable.

IF A MUTUAL FUND HAS THIS COMBINATION OF FEES...				...HERE'S WHAT $2,000 EARNING 5% A YEAR WOULD BE WORTH AFTER:			
FRONT-END LOAD	12b-1 FEE	ANNUAL EXPENSES	EXIT FEE	1 YEAR	3 YEARS	5 YEARS	10 YEARS
0%	0%	0.75%	0%	$2,084	$2,264	$2,458	$3,021
0	0.75	1.75	0	2,047	2,146	2,249	2,529
2	0	1.25	1	2,032	2,185	2,349	2,780
4	0	0.75	0	2,001	2,173	2,360	2,901
4	0.25	1.75	0	1,976	2,092	2,215	2,555
7	0	0.75	0	1,938	2,015	2,286	2,810

in funds you already own—assuming, of course, that they're good per-formers—makes more sense than buying shares in a new fund each time you have money to invest. As many investors have learned, it's easy to get carried away and end up owning shares in an unmanageable number of different funds.

Unless you have psychic powers or are extraordinarily lucky, you might as well forget about trying to buy fund shares when their prices are at their lowest or about selling when they reach the pinnacle. In fact, human psychology being what it is, many investors end up buying when prices are high (thinking they'll go higher) and selling when they're low (fearful that they'll fall further).

For most people, the smartest way to invest in mutual funds is through a regular series of investments. The best known of these strat-egies is called dollar-cost averaging, and it works like this: Each month (or week or other regular interval), you invest a set amount of money, regardless of what the fund's share price is at that moment.

Dollar-cost averaging devotees will point out that because you're investing the same amount each time, you'll receive more shares when the share price is low and fewer shares when it's high, resulting in a lower-than-average share price over time. While that's true, the real strength of dollar-cost averaging lies in the discipline it imposes on investors to invest regularly. Investing, like exercise and many other tasks, is a lot easier if you can make it a habit.

To make regular investing even less arduous, some fund companies offer automatic investment plans. Each month (or any time period you choose), they will draw money out of your bank account to buy fund shares. Other fund companies will automatically transfer money from your money-market mutual fund at that same fund company into, say, one of their stock funds. Your employer may also allow you to invest in the mutual fund of your choice through regular payroll deductions.

In choosing a fund for a dollar-cost averaging program, look for one that doesn't require a minimum subsequent investment that's greater than the amount you plan to invest. Most funds require minimum sub-sequent investments in the $100 to $250 range. Also look for a fund that doesn't charge a load each time you invest. While there may be some tiny amount of logic in paying a load to buy a fund initially (if you need a salesperson's advice on which fund to buy), there's no point throwing away as much as 8.5 percent of all the money you invest later.

INVESTING A LUMP SUM

At some point in your life, you may come into a large amount of money that you will want to invest. It may, for example, be an inheritance or the profit on the sale of your home.

The first thing to do is to give yourself some time to think. Park the money in a safe place, such as federally insured short-term certificates-of-deposit at the bank, while you work out your investing plans. If your newfound fortune totals more than $100,000, you should probably split it among several banks so you don't exceed the limits on federal deposit insurance coverage.

Next, consider where and how to invest your money. If you're already following an asset-allocation strategy that you're satisfied with, you may want to divide your new money among the mutual funds already in your portfolio. (If you don't have an asset-allocation plan but are interested in developing one, see chapter 4.)

When you're ready to invest, resist the understandable impulse to write one big check and get it over with. A regular series of investments, applying the simple tactic known as dollar-cost averaging, will help protect you from the danger of investing everything at the worst possible moment. With a very large sum of money, you may want to take as long as two years to become fully invested.

Even in the case of smaller lump sums, dollar-cost averaging may be your shrewdest move. How many separate investments you'll be able to make with your money will depend, of course, on the minimum investment each fund will accept (usually $100 to $250). If you plan to buy into a particular fund for the first time, you'll also need to satisfy an initial investment minimum, usually of at least $1,000 and often as high as $2,500 or $3,000.

WHEN YOU SHOULDN'T BUY

There is at least one time when you should avoid putting money into a mutual fund, and that is right before the fund declares a distribution. Most funds distribute capital gains and other income once a year, often in mid- to late December but sometimes in earlier months. In simple terms, capital gains are the profits that the fund made during the year by selling securities for more than it paid for them.

When the distribution is paid out to shareholders, the price of a fund's shares will fall accordingly. You can usually arrange to receive the distribution in cash or have it automatically reinvested in more shares of the fund.

Here's where the problem comes in. Suppose you invested $1,000 on December 15 in a fund with a share price of $10. You received 100 shares. Then, on December 18 the fund declared a distribution of $1 per share. The shares you paid $10 for are now worth $9 each, or a total of $900. If you have your distribution automatically reinvested, the remaining $100 will buy you more shares at the new price of $9. Otherwise, you will receive your $100 in the form of a check. Either way, you still have $1,000, but now (unless the money was in a tax-deferred account) you owe tax on $100 of it. Because you owned the fund for only a few days and the fund's capital gains were, in all likelihood, earned earlier in the year, you will have to pay tax on profits you never enjoyed.

To avoid this tax trap, simply call the fund to ask when it plans to make its distributions. If you have money you must, for one reason or another, invest at the end of the year, consider putting it first in a money-market fund in the same family as the fund you ultimately plan to invest in. After the fund makes its distribution, you can transfer the money from your money-market fund, usually with just a phone call.

INVESTING FOR COLLEGE

If you have college-bound children (or if you're college-bound yourself), you're probably well acquainted with those scary projections of what college is likely to cost in some far-off year. By one recent estimate, for example, four years at a private university for a child born in 1991 is likely to cost $290,000—or even more.

Next to planning for retirement, investing for college may be the most daunting financial challenge the average family will face. And like retirement planning, the task is far easier the sooner you begin.

First, bear in mind that the picture isn't quite as bad as the gigantic numbers might lead you to believe. According to the College Board, about half of all students in postsecondary education receive some sort of financial aid. The aid may take forms such as grants, scholarships, work-study programs, or relatively low interest loans. Much of that aid is available to middle-income families as well as to those with lower incomes.

But if a decade's worth of loan-payment coupons don't strike you as the ideal college graduation present, then you'll want to begin an investment plan to pay as much of the tab as possible. There are a number of investments that offer special inducements for college savers.

U.S. Savings Bonds, for example, earn interest tax-free under certain conditions, if they're ultimately used to pay college or vocational-school tuition and fees. The bonds must be in a parent's name, and there are restrictions on how much income the parents can have at the time the bonds are redeemed. Above a certain income, the interest is no longer tax-deductible. You can find out more about this program at banks that sell savings bonds.

Many mutual fund companies also have special programs for college saving. In general, they work like this: First, you make an initial investment of a certain minimum amount into the fund of your choice. (Some funds set lower minimums for these accounts than they do for conventional ones.) At the same time, you commit to making a series of regular investments in the fund, such as through automatic monthly withdrawals from your checking account. As your child nears college age, some fund companies have programs to begin systematic withdrawals from, say, the growth-stock fund you chose earlier, with the money going into a less risky money-market fund. Then, you can write checks on your money-market fund to pay the bills as they come due.

In Whose Name Should the Account Be Established?

You can set up a college fund either in your name or in your child's name. Having it in your name has several advantages. One is that your child may qualify for more financial aid, since some financial-aid formulas put more weight on a child's assets than on a parent's. Another advantage is that by having the account in your name, you have greater control over how the money will be used. Otherwise, the money you patiently saved to send your child to NYU may instead go to BMW.

Putting the money in your child's name has its own set of advantages. Primarily, you'll have to pay less tax on the investment earnings over the years, which should mean that the account will grow faster.

You can put money in a child's name either through a trust or through a custodial account.

While a trust can be costlier to start and maintain than a custodial account, it may make sense if you plan to put a lot of money in a child's name or if you want to keep some control over how and when your child gets hold of it. To set up a trust, you'll probably need to hire a lawyer knowledgeable in estate planning.

You can open a custodial account in the name of a child, under either the Uniform Gifts to Minors Act or the Uniform Transfers to Minors Act, depending on the state where you live. UGMA accounts and UTMA accounts are similar, though UTMA accounts can be used to shelter more types of assets from taxation. Either is well suited for mutual funds, and the fund company you choose can supply you with all the essential paperwork.

If your child is under age 14, the first $600 (as of 1993) of unearned income he or she receives will not be subject to federal income tax. Unearned income means the income from an investment, rather than from a job, and includes dividends, interest, and capital gains. The tax-free figure, in this case $600, is periodically adjusted for inflation.

Currently, if your child receives more than $600 in unearned income, the next $600 will be taxed at the child's tax rate, usually 15 percent. Unearned income above $1,200 will be taxed at the parent's top marginal rate.

When your child turns 14, a new set of rules apply. At that point, all income the child receives will be taxed at the child's tax rate, usually 15 percent.

Choosing the Right Funds

In recent times, college costs have increased faster than the overall inflation rate, typically rising 8 to 9 percent each year. For your college fund to do its job, the investments you choose for it will have to beat the college inflation rate, at a minimum. The mutual funds most likely to do that, if history is any guide, are stock funds. (Chapter 2 explains the various types of stock funds and how they work.) For college investing, any of the following types of stock funds may be appropriate, depending on how comfortable you are with risk: aggressive-growth,

growth, growth-and-income, stock index, or international stock. You might also want to hedge your bets by splitting your money into several accounts—for example, one U.S. stock fund and one international stock fund.

As your child nears college age, you should gradually shift some of your money into less risky funds to avoid the danger of having to sell your stock funds when the stock market is at a low point. Either a money-market fund or a short-term bond fund would be an appropriate choice for that purpose. But it's probably not a good idea to bail out of the stock market entirely come freshman year. If the costs for college continue to grow at a rapid rate, they could eat away a substantial portion of your portfolio's value by the time you sit down to write those senior-year tuition checks.

Investing for college can serve another practical purpose beyond paying tuition bills. Over the years, your child will have an opportunity to learn some real-world lessons about managing money. That can be an education in itself, and a priceless one.

SHOULD YOU MIX INSURANCE AND MUTUAL FUNDS?

One type of life insurance allows policyholders to invest some of their policy's cash value in certain mutual funds. It's called variable life.

Insurance companies promote variable life as a way for policyholders to exercise more control over how their money is invested, while enjoying tax-deferral on their investment earnings until the money is withdrawn. That's true, as far as it goes.

But variable life also shifts the investment risk from the insurance company to the policyholder. With other types of cash-value policies, the insurance company decides how to invest the money and bears most of the risk.

A variable life policy's death benefit (the amount your beneficiaries will receive when you die) can vary from year to year, depending on how well the investment account performs. The policy's cash-surrender value (the amount you'd receive if you dropped the policy) may also be tied to the ups and downs of the investment account.

Some policies do guarantee a minimum death benefit, and some offer a guaranteed interest option that will credit a minimum rate of interest, usually 4 percent, to the cash-surrender value each year. However, those provisions may not guarantee as much insurance coverage as you need at a price that you can afford.

Consumers Union believes that for most people, mixing life insurance protection with investment speculation is a recipe for disappointment. The goal of life insurance is to provide enough money for your family if you die while they still need your support. Tying your death benefit to the performance of the investment markets may result in your beneficiaries receiving less money than they need or, in a good year, more. The latter prospect might be appealing, but the former prospect isn't a risk worth taking, in our view. So unless you already have additional life insurance or other financial assets to meet your survivors' financial needs, avoid variable life.

WHY FUNDS CLOSE TO NEW INVESTORS

Sometimes, in your search for the right mutual fund, you'll come across one that is no longer accepting money from new investors. Funds close for a variety of reasons, but the most common one is that the manager decides the fund is getting too big, too fast. Bigger isn't always better for certain types of mutual funds. A fund that focuses on small, rapidly growing companies, for example, may have difficulty finding enough good ones to buy stock in if it suddenly receives a huge influx of cash from investors. That can easily happen when a formerly obscure fund appears atop a national magazine's list of hot funds.

If you're interested in a particular fund but read that it has closed, call the fund to make sure. When closed funds reopen, it's often without the publicity that attended their closing. Some otherwise closed funds will also remain open to new IRA accounts.

If you already own shares in a closed fund, you can usually continue to contribute to your account. But don't assume it's a superior performer just because it isn't letting anyone else in. To merit your continued confidence, it should still hold its own against other funds of its type. Otherwise you may want to consider selling, just as you would with any other fund you own. The door to that fund may be barred on the outside, but fortunately, you can still get out if you wish.

Finally, don't feel left out if you can't get in a certain fund. In early

1993, after a rash of fund closings, fewer than 50 stock and bond funds were officially closed. With some 4,000 funds in the marketplace, that represented little more than 1 percent of all funds. However good closed funds may be, there are still many fine funds that would welcome a new account with your name on it. (Several funds that were closed at the time of *Consumer Reports'* most recent study are noted in the Ratings in chapter 9; some of them may have since reopened. Other funds in the Ratings, open at the time of our study, may be closed when you read this.)

Should You Buy a Brand-New Fund?

Conventional financial wisdom cautions against buying a mutual fund before it has been around for a few years and established a solid performance record. Consumer Reports *excludes funds that haven't been in existence for at least five years from its fund Ratings for that very reason.*

Nevertheless, as a fund investor, you can expect to be besieged with advertising for new funds. Should you ever take up the offer? The answer depends on a few considerations.

First, and most basic, what does the fund invest in? If it's an investment that makes sense to you, and one that isn't already covered by a fund with an established record, perhaps the new fund is worth a look.

Second, does the fund offer any special inducements to early investors? For example, it might normally impose a sales charge, or load, on investments but drop those charges for the first year. Or, it might reduce its management fee for a limited period of time to make its returns more attractive.

Any such concessions on the part of a new fund can make it seem like a bargain. Bear in mind, though, that once the new-investor honeymoon is over, the fund will reinstate its load, so you'll wind up paying commissions on your subsequent invest-ments. And when its full management fees are restored, you'll have to pay those, too.

A final consideration: Just how many funds do you want to own? Each fund you add to your portfolio will mean time and paperwork on your part. Whether you buy brand-new funds or venerable ones, your best strategy will be to build a sufficiently diversified portfolio and keep adding money to the funds you already have.

4 HOW TO BUILD A PORTFOLIO OF FUNDS

"'Tis the part of a wise man . . . not [to] venture all his eggs in one basket."

—Cervantes

"Put all your eggs in one basket and—watch the basket."

—Mark Twain

Miguel de Cervantes would probably have made a better mutual fund investor than Mark Twain. He obviously had a handle on the concept of diversification. But Twain, too, had a point. Wherever you decide to invest your fund money, you'll want to keep a sharp eye on it.

THE BIG PICTURE

At certain points in life—when you apply for a college loan or a home mortgage, for example—you'll probably be asked to prepare a net worth statement. Before you begin a program of investing in mutual funds, you may want to go through that exercise for your own benefit. Mutual funds, after all, are likely to represent only a portion of all the things you own.

Preparing a net worth statement will give you a quick picture of how much money you already have and where it is. Use the list below to figure your approximate net worth. If you don't have exact figures at hand, just make your best guess.

First, list your assets and how much each is worth:

checking accounts	$_____
savings accounts	_____
certificates-of-deposit	_____
U.S. Savings Bonds	_____
cash value of life insurance	_____
stocks	_____
bonds	_____
mutual funds	_____
retirement plans	_____
your home's current market value (if you own it)	_____
other real estate	_____
cars and other personal property	_____
antiques and collectibles	_____
your business (if you own one or part of one)	_____
other assets	_____
Total assets	$_____

Next, list your liabilities and assign a dollar figure to each:

mortgage(s)	$_____
home equity loans	_____
student loans	_____
car loans	_____
credit-card debts	_____
other debts	_____
Total liabilities	$_____

Now subtract your total liabilities from your total assets. The result is your **net worth.**

$_____

LESSONS IN LIQUIDITY

There are any number of things you can learn from a net worth statement that will be useful in planning your mutual fund investing. One is how liquid, or easily cashed in, your savings and investments are. Whatever money you have in the bank (except for long-term CDs, which may carry penalties if cashed in early) counts as liquid, as does a money-market mutual fund account.

Stocks, bonds, and mutual funds of stocks and bonds can also be sold quickly. But unlike the other liquid investments, they go up and down in value. So you run the risk of selling them at a low price if you must cash them in quickly. You may want to think of them as semi-liquid.

Some investments are so far from liquid that you might as well think of them as solids. Your home can turn out to be a fine long-term investment, but it could take months or even years to sell. The same is true for a business you may own. Any money you have in a pension plan is also difficult to tap quickly or without substantial penalties.

It is advisable to have at least enough money in liquid investments to cover your current bills plus an emergency fund. Your emergency fund ideally should be large enough to cover three to six months of living expenses, depending on whether you have one wage earner or more in your household. Families with more than one wage earner can get by with a smaller emergency fund, because they'll still have some money coming in if one family member loses a job.

If you're short of liquid assets, consider setting up an account at, for example, a money-market mutual fund. Then, make regular deposits until you have enough money set aside. Once your emergency fund is adequate, you can begin to think about more speculative investments.

Of course, you may also discover from your net worth statement that you have more money in the bank and other liquid accounts than you need to have. That could mean that you're giving up potential investment returns for no good reason. In that case, it's time to consider moving some of that money into investments with better long-term prospects, such as carefully chosen stock mutual funds.

A BALANCING ACT

Your net worth statement can also tell you whether you have too much of one type of investment and too little of another. You can then use your mutual fund investments to bring your portfolio into better balance.

For example, you may already own some stocks. That could mean you won't need to put as much money into stock funds as you would if you owned no stocks at all. But you should also take a look at what those stocks are. If you own conservative stocks, such as shares of public utility companies, you might want to choose a mutual fund that invests in other types of companies with greater growth potential. If you own a lot of stock in one company, such as the one you work for, you may want to sell some of it and invest the proceeds in a diversified mutual fund. As a general rule, you probably shouldn't have any more than 10 percent of your money tied up in the stock of any single company.

Similarly, if you already have money invested in bonds, you may not want to put as much money into bond funds as you otherwise would. And if you own your home, a real estate mutual fund might be an unnecessary addition to your portfolio. As you review the asset-allocation models in this chapter, remember that mutual funds can be an important part of your assets—perhaps the most important part—but they aren't the entire picture.

DESIGNING YOUR PERSONAL PORTFOLIO

There's no such thing, alas, as a one-size-fits-all portfolio. But advice on the subject is plentiful. Financial books and magazines are filled with pie charts showing how people at different stages of life should invest their holdings. Brokerage firms and investment advisers have their own formulas.

Let's look at several ways to invest your money that have been presented in the pages of *Consumer Reports* in recent years. They range from a crude (but perhaps effective) scheme to a sophisticated asset-allocation model firmly rooted in historical research.

We'll begin with the crude model:

1. Subtract your age from 100.
2. Put that percentage of your money into stock funds.
3. Put the rest into bond funds (minus 10 percent for money-market funds).
4. The end.

As simplistic as that model is, it does address the key question you'll have to consider in designing your portfolio: How much risk can you afford to take with your money? In general, the younger you are, the more risks you can take in pursuit of greater investment returns. If an investment goes sour, you'll have more years to earn the money back. But if you're retired, or nearing retirement, you'll have less time to catch up. Perhaps more important, you may no longer have the earning power to replenish your investment funds.

However, age isn't the only thing that determines how much risk you can take. Another factor to consider is how soon you may need the money. An enterprising eighth-grader investing for college will need to begin withdrawing money for tuition bills in four or five years. A young couple may be saving toward the down payment on a house 10 years into the future. A 65-year-old retiree with a good pension and Social Security income may have fund accounts he or she doesn't expect to tap for at least another decade.

You'll also have to consider another important variable that cuts across age groups: how comfortable you are with the possibility that you may lose money. Mutual funds fluctuate in value, often daily. To choose the most vivid example in recent memory, when the stock market crashed in October 1987, investors suffered losses, at least on paper, of more than 24 percent. In a mutual fund that fell 24 percent in value, an account worth $2,000 one day was worth just $1,520 the next. The stock market soon rebounded and has amply rewarded investors who held on to their shares. But many other investors, made queasy by the crash and fearful of further declines, had already sold. Their losses weren't merely on paper; they were real money.

The stock market may crash again someday. It will certainly have its ups and downs. And some mutual funds will lose value for other reasons as well, including bad investment decisions by their managers. But anyone who shies away from investing in mutual funds out of fear should be aware of a risk that's at least as real and, in some ways, more insidious than the vicissitudes of the stock market. That risk is inflation.

Inflation erodes the future purchasing power of money. When inflation is running at the relatively modest rate of 3 percent, a dollar today will be worth only about 97 cents next year. So next year, a dollar would buy you only what 97 cents would have bought you this year. In 10 years, if inflation stays constant at 3 percent a year, a dollar would be worth about 74 cents.

As inflation speeds up, the future becomes an ever more expensive place in which to live. As recently as 1981, inflation in the United States was running at an annual rate of more than 10 percent, as measured by the Consumer Price Index.

For any investment to be worth more tomorrow than it is worth today, in real dollar terms, it must first perform better than the inflation rate. From 1988 to 1992, inflation ran at an average annual rate of about 4.3 percent. Here is how some common investments did during that same time period.

	AVERAGE ANNUAL RETURN
Common stocks	16%
Corporate bonds	11
Government bonds	10
Treasury bills	6

Of course, as we noted earlier, those five years were good ones for stocks and for bonds, as well. Stocks, in particular, can lose money in any given year. But this five-year period isn't out of line with the general trend. Over time, stocks have proven more adept than other investments at staying ahead of inflation. Treasury bills, while providing the ultimate in safety, have barely outpaced inflation. If you're in a high enough tax bracket, you can even lose money, once inflation is figured in, by investing in Treasury bills.

A more sophisticated approach to devising a portfolio is shown in Table 4.1 from the American Association of Individual Investors. It shows six different ways of splitting up a portfolio based on two variables: your distance from retirement and your appetite for risk. The column headed "Cash" refers to liquid investments such as money-market mutual funds.

Note that even conservative investors at retirement should have at

TABLE 4.1   PORTFOLIOS FOR THE CONSERVATIVE AND THE AGGRESSIVE

IF YOU ARE...	STOCKS	BONDS	CASH
Five or more years from retirement			
and conservative	40%	40%	20%
and aggressive	60%	30%	10%
Close to retirement			
and conservative	30%	50%	20%
and aggressive	50%	40%	10%
At retirement			
and conservative	20%	60%	20%
and aggressive	40%	50%	10%

Source: American Association of Individual Investors, 625 North Michigan Avenue, Chicago, IL 60611

least 20 percent of their money in stocks, according to this table. The reason, again, is inflation. Though you may not think of stocks as conservative investments, a portfolio with no stocks at all would be hard-pressed to stay safely ahead of inflation over the long run. And even investors of retirement age are likely to be in the race against inflation for a considerable length of time.

Table 4.2 is considerably more involved. It's based on the concept of asset allocation, which has recently become a popular phrase in the world of mutual funds. Some financial advisers use it simply as a fancy synonym for diversification. There is even a category of mutual funds that call themselves asset-allocation funds.

Basically, asset allocation is an investing strategy based on the historical performance of various types of investments. The idea is to divide, or "allocate," your assets in predetermined proportions among those investments. The different investments will do well at different times. But, theoretically, if your portfolio is properly constructed, the general trend should be steadily upward.

Table 4.2 shows three asset-allocation models, based on different levels of risk. They were adapted for *Consumer Reports* by Roger C. Gibson, president of a Pittsburgh-based money management firm and author of a 1990 book on asset-allocation techniques. All but two of the

TABLE 4.2 ALLOCATING YOUR ASSETS

These three portfolios vary their allocations according to how much risk the investor is comfortable taking. In theory at least, the higher-risk portfolio should outperform the lower-risk portfolio over the long term. Investors whose portfolios are not yet large enough to slice into this many pieces can still enjoy some of the benefits of asset allocation by diversifying among the asset categories that are marked with an asterisk (*).

	PERCENT ALLOCATED		
ASSET CATEGORY	LOWER-RISK PORTFOLIO	MEDIUM-RISK PORTFOLIO	HIGHER-RISK PORTFOLIO
FIXED-VALUE	**35%**	**22%**	**6%**
* Money-market funds	10.0%	10.0%	6.0%
CDs	12.5	6.0	0.0
GICs[1]	12.5	6.0	0.0
BONDS	**35%**	**33%**	**29%**
* Short-term	20.0	15.0	9.0
Intermediate-term[2]			
* higher quality	6.0	7.2	8.0
lower quality	3.0	3.6	4.0
Foreign	6.0	7.2	8.0
EQUITIES	**30%**	**45%**	**65%**
Convertible securities	2.0	3.0	4.3
* Large company U.S. stocks	4.0	6.0	8.7
* Small company U.S. stocks	6.0	9.0	13.0
* Foreign stocks	8.0	12.0	17.0
Real estate securities	7.0	10.0	15.0
Gold mining stocks	3.0	5.0	7.0

[1]Guaranteed investment contracts, available only through employer-sponsored retirement savings plans.
[2]Bonds maturing in five to nine years.
Source: Reprinted with permission of the author, Roger C. Gibson, from *Asset Allocation: Balancing Financial Risk,* published by Business-One Irwin, Copyright © 1990.

investments referred to in the table (CDs and GICs) are available through mutual funds.

To follow one of the asset-allocation models in Table 4.2, you would need a portfolio of at least five mutual funds plus a money-market fund. Those funds are marked with an asterisk (*).

You would not, of course, have to buy all the funds at once. You could, instead, first buy the funds that least resemble the assets you already have, as listed earlier in your net worth statement. Then you could buy the remaining funds as money became available.

Whether or not you elect to follow the table's guidelines in developing your portfolio, there are several useful lessons to be learned from it. First, all three portfolios have some money invested in stocks. Even the lower-risk portfolio, if you add up the entries with and without asterisks, has 30 percent of its money in stocks and other equity investments.

Second, none of the portfolios would put more than 12.5 percent in guaranteed investment contracts, commonly known as GICs. The simplified models marked by the asterisks would omit GICs entirely. GICs are contracts sold by insurance companies through employer-sponsored retirement plans. They promise to pay a certain rate of interest over the term of the contract, such as one to five years. They have been, in recent times, the single most popular investment choice of people in 401(k) retirement plans, far surpassing stock and bond mutual funds, for example. That may prove unfortunate for tomorrow's retirees. Although GICs are generally considered safe, they're unlikely to generate the sort of returns that will keep an investor well ahead of future inflation.

Third, note that all three models call for some investment in foreign securities (though only foreign stocks made the cut for the asterisked models). In today's world, even a low-risk investor should consider having some money invested internationally, and mutual funds are the easiest way to do that.

Finally, note that the models call for investing in short- and intermediate-term bonds, but not in long-term bonds. Many professional investors believe that long-term bonds don't adequately compensate investors for the risks involved in tying up their money for a long period. Intermediate-term bonds pay nearly as much interest, but tie up your money for considerably less time.

HOW MANY FUNDS SHOULD YOU OWN?

As you build your portfolio of funds over the years, try to guard against the temptation to invest in too many funds. That isn't always easy. Fund companies are constantly coming up with new types of funds, and the sales pitches can be persuasive. But remember, the more funds you own, the harder they will be to keep track of, the more paperwork you'll face, and the more hassles you'll inflict on your heirs.

What is the right number of funds to own? The asset-allocation model would suggest a minimum of five, plus a money-market fund. *Consumer Reports* also put that question to a random sample of readers who invest in funds. Their median answer: four.

Four or five funds is probably a manageable number for most people. You may, of course, want to own more than that number, as many investors do. Some serious investors want a more diversified portfolio than any four or five funds can provide. To build a portfolio modeled on the full version of the asset-allocation table, for example, you'd need to own nine funds, plus a money-market fund. Other investors enjoy following their funds as a hobby and are happy to devote hours every week to charting their ups and downs. So there can be good reasons for owning more than four or five funds, just as there are bad ones.

FOLLOWING YOUR FUNDS

The prices of mutual funds are easy to track. Most daily newspapers publish tables in their business pages that show what each fund was worth at the close of business on the previous day. You probably won't want to look up your funds every day. In fact, if you're likely to be bothered by short-term declines, checking prices every day can be disconcerting.

You shouldn't, however, just buy a fund and forget it, particularly if you're saving toward a specific goal. If you wait until you need to cash in your investments before checking on your fund's progress, you may be in for a surprise.

You can buy computer software to keep track of your mutual funds, or you can devise a simple low-tech system. There is no one best method, so do whatever you're comfortable with.

One easy way to keep track of your funds is simply to list them alphabetically on a sheet of notepaper. Write down how many shares you own according to the most recent statement you received from the fund. Then write down the current share price, as reported in your newspaper. Multiply the number of shares by the price per share for the current value of your fund. You can then total the results for each separate fund to determine the value of your whole fund portfolio.

To keep track of your fund statements with a minimum of effort, file them alphabetically by fund name in a loose-leaf binder. Use dividers to separate funds, and put the most recent statements on top as you receive them. Since some fund statements will cover overlapping time periods, you can go through your binder periodically and weed out statements you don't need. Be sure, though, to keep a record of what you originally paid for fund shares; you will need that information at tax time if you eventually sell your shares.

5 MUTUAL FUNDS FOR RETIREMENT PLANNING

It's never too soon to begin thinking about retirement, even if today is your first day on your first job. The earlier you get started, the easier it will be to reach your goals—though you may not have a clue yet as to what those goals will be.

If you're well along in your career and haven't done much thinking about retirement, there's no reason to despair—or to put it off any longer. You may be at or near your peak earning years right now, and you probably have far more disposable income than you did in years past. You'll just have to dispose of less of that income and begin investing it as productively as possible.

HOW MUCH WILL YOU NEED?

Many financial advisers say that in retirement most people will need an income that equals about 80 percent of their take-home pay before they retired. For example, if you earned $40,000 a year and paid $11,000 in taxes (for an after-tax income of $29,000), you would need about 80 percent of $29,000, or $23,200.

You, of course, may need more or less than 80 percent depending on the sort of retirement you envision for yourself. If you want to make a more precise estimate, list all the expenses you expect to have in retirement and add them up. An easy way to do that is to start with a list of all the things you now spend money on. Then, try to predict what you'll spend on each item in retirement. Some expenses will decline once you retire, while others will rise. For example, you're likely to spend far less on business clothes and commuting, but you may spend more on health care and travel.

Most people draw on a number of sources for their retirement income: Social Security benefits, employer pensions, and their own retirement savings. In 1993, by *Consumer Reports'* estimate, those first two income sources (Social Security and pensions) account for about 60 percent of the average retiree's income. The rest comes from personal savings.

Table 5.1 shows one estimate of how much money people with different incomes may need to save toward their retirement. As you can see from the notes at the bottom of the chart, we had to make many different assumptions in order to come up with the numbers. Those include such unpredictable variables as the average rate of inflation for the next 10, 20, or 30 years. So consider this table only an approximation, a tool to help you in thinking about your future retirement needs.

In reading about retirement planning, you're likely to come across countless charts and worksheets that will try to help you estimate how much money you will need when you retire. They can, as we say, be useful tools, but don't be lulled into a false sense of security by their apparent precision. Too many things can change between now and the time you retire. Pension laws are amended year after year. The Social Security system is the subject of an ongoing political debate. And inflation, which may have a greater impact on your financial needs in retirement than anything else, remains stubbornly unpredictable. Perhaps the best advice, if the hardest to follow, is to put away as much money as you can for retirement and try to invest that money as productively as possible, without making yourself miserable in the meantime.

Figuring Your Social Security Benefits

You can obtain an estimate of your future Social Security benefits by calling the Social Security Administration at 800-772-1213. You'll

TABLE 5.1   HOW MUCH TO SAVE?

The middle column shows how much money you are likely to need at retirement
to supplement your Social Security benefits if you have no other source of
retirement income. The column at right shows how much you would need to
invest each year before you retire in order to reach that goal.

YOUR CURRENT INCOME	SAVINGS NEEDED AT RETIREMENT	ANNUAL INVESTMENT NEEDED
	10 years to retirement	
$30,000	$107,331	$7,902
40,000	170,374	12,543
60,000	389,151	28,649
	20 years to retirement	
$30,000	$158,821	$4,317
40,000	252,108	6,853
60,000	575,838	15,654
	30 years to retirement	
$30,000	$234,968	$3,075
40,000	372,982	4,881
60,000	851,926	11,143

Other assumptions: Savings invested in taxable accounts. Average annual inflation is 4 percent, annual
rate of return is 8 percent. Retirement at age 65, retirement period of 25 years. Retirement income at
80 percent of after-tax, preretirement income, 28 percent federal tax rate; no state tax. Projected Social
Security benefit based on current benefits for each income example: $11,892 for $30,000, $12,768 for
$40,000, and $13,536 for $60,000.

Source: T. Rowe Price Associates, Inc.

need to fill out an application form and send it in. What you'll eventually receive is a Personal Earnings and Benefit Statement. *Consumer
Reports* found that this process, from start to finish, takes about four to
six weeks.

The statement shows what you can expect to receive in future
Social Security benefits (expressed in today's dollars) when you retire. It
also shows what you would receive if you were to become disabled and
what your survivors would receive if you were to die.

Aside from aiding you in your retirement planning, requesting one
of these estimates every couple of years is a good way to make sure your
Social Security records are in proper order. If you find an error, you
should try to have it corrected as soon as possible.

Predicting Your Pension

There are two basic types of pension plans: defined-benefit plans and defined-contribution plans. An employer may offer one or both types, or neither.

In a defined-benefit plan, your employer invests money to fund your future pension. Such an arrangement is called a defined-benefit plan because the amount you will receive (the benefit) is specified (defined) in your pension plan. It is your employer's responsibility to make sure that the money is there when you need it.

In a defined-contribution plan, all that is defined is the contribution, that is, the money you and possibly your employer put in. How much money you will have in the plan when you retire will depend on how successfully it was invested over the years. A well-known example of a defined-contribution plan, one you may have at work, is called a 401(k) plan.

Defined-benefit plans are increasingly rare. A 1989 Labor Department study showed that the number of defined-benefit plans in the United States declined from 170,000 to 146,000 between 1985 and 1988. The number of defined-contribution plans rose during the same period from 462,000 to 584,000. The upshot of this trend is that future retirees must take greater responsibility for how their pension money is invested, whether they want to or not. Often, their choice will be among several mutual funds and the guaranteed investment contracts (GICs) sold by insurance companies.

Your Savings and Investments

In the most general sense, there are two ways to save and invest for retirement: at work, through a program sponsored by your employer; and on your own.

INVESTING AT WORK

If you have a defined-benefit pension plan, you may have no investment decisions to worry about. It's your employer's job to make sure the money is properly invested and that the monthly retirement benefit you've been promised will be there when you retire.

If you have a defined-contribution plan, the investment choices generally are yours to make, from among the options offered to you by your employer. The most common types of defined contribution plans are the 401(k) plan are the 403(b) plan, both named after the sections of the U.S. tax code that established them.

How 401(k) and 403(b) Plans Work

The 401(k) plan is generally for employees of for-profit businesses. You tell your employer how much of your salary you want to contribute. Your employer withholds that money from your paycheck, and your taxable income is reduced by a like amount. The money your 401(k) investments earn over the years is not subject to income tax until you withdraw it. State and local income taxes are generally deferred, too.

Your employer may match some or all of your contribution. For that reason, many financial advisers suggest contributing at least enough money to a 401(k) plan to obtain the maximum employer match. If your employer will match, say, 3 percent of your salary, that's essentially a 3 percent raise, yours for the asking.

The maximum allowable pretax contribution changes each year, to reflect the rise in the Consumer Price Index. In 1994 the maximum was $9,240.

If your plan allows, you may also be able to make additional contributions with after-tax dollars. The investment earnings on those contributions will also not be subject to tax until you withdraw them. (For the purposes of this book, we will be discussing primarily 401(k) plans that are funded with pretax contributions.)

Because of new rules that took effect in 1993, your employer may offer you at least three substantially different investment choices. Your employer may, of course, offer many more than that. Those choices may include your company's stock, the guaranteed investment contracts sold by insurance companies, and various types of mutual funds.

You may begin withdrawing money from your 401(k) after you retire or, generally, after you reach age 59½. (You *must* begin to withdraw after you reach the age of 70½.) You may be able to withdraw money earlier than age 59½ if you become disabled. Early withdrawals may also be allowed in the case of certain narrowly defined financial emergencies; such withdrawals are, however, subject to strict rules and tax penalties. So it's best to think of a 401(k) as a long-term commitment and to choose your mutual funds or other investments accordingly.

Depending on the rules set by your employer, you may be able to borrow money from your 401(k) plan. The amount you may borrow can't exceed half the value of your vested account, or $50,000, whichever is less. The interest rate will be based on current market rates. The money must be paid back, typically within five years. And if you leave your employer before the loan has been repaid, you may have to promptly repay the full loan balance.

When you leave an employer, you have several choices about what to do with your 401(k) account. You can leave it where it is, if your former employer permits. That may make sense if you were satisfied with your investment choices and the way your former employer administered the plan. You may also be able to put the money in a 401(k) plan at your new workplace, if your new employer allows. Finally, you can put the money in a rollover IRA at, for example, a mutual fund company.

If you choose the IRA route, note that a 1993 change in the tax rules requires employers to withhold 20 percent of any money you receive as part of a retirement account distribution. If you roll over the entire distribution (including enough money to make up for the 20 percent that was withheld), the withheld portion will be refunded to you after you file your tax return for the year. You can avoid withholding—and the rest of this rigmarole—if you have the money moved directly from your former employer's plan to your new employer's plan or to a rollover IRA, without taking possession of it yourself.

Note that rolling over a lump-sum distribution from a retirement plan into an IRA also affects your eligibility to use a technique called forward-averaging to reduce your income tax liability in retirement. So you may want to consult a tax adviser or your company's pension administrator before proceeding.

The 403(b) plan resembles the 401(k) plan in many particulars. It is usually available to employees of schools, hospitals, and certain other nonprofit organizations. One key difference is that you may be able to contribute more money to a 403(b) than to a 401(k), especially after you have worked for that employer for a certain number of years.

Other Options

Your employer may offer other ways to invest money, not specifically for retirement. For example, you may be able to arrange for automatic investments in a mutual fund each pay period. Mutual funds that offer automatic investing plans can provide you with the necessary forms. Funds often require lower minimum investments if you sign up for automatic withdrawals than if you were simply to send in a check every now and then. You may, for example, be able to contribute as little as $25 per paycheck to the fund you choose.

The money you set aside in this manner won't have the tax advantages of a retirement plan, but at least it will be invested and, with any luck, it will be growing in value. And unlike most retirement accounts, such money is yours to tap as needed and without tax penalties.

INVESTING ON YOUR OWN

You can save for retirement outside of the workplace, through tax-deferred vehicles such as IRAs or through investments without any special tax status. In general, you'll do best to put your long-term investment money first into tax-deferred accounts, because it will grow the fastest there.

Should You Have an IRA?

When Individual Retirement Accounts, or IRAs, were made widely available in 1982, they represented a relatively easy way for the average working American to save toward retirement. An individual could put aside $2,000 each year and both that $2,000 and its subsequent investment earnings would not be subject to income tax until the money was withdrawn during retirement.

The tax reform act of 1986 greatly complicated the IRA rules, making IRAs less attractive for some people, and scaring off others for whom an IRA might still be a good deal. At this writing, there is talk of further IRA reforms. But here are the rules as they stand in 1993.

The basic rules. Anyone who earns $2,000 in a given year may still invest $2,000 in an IRA. Spouses who each earn at least $2,000 may each put $2,000 in an IRA. A couple with only one income may invest $2,250 between them.

IRA contributions are still tax-deductible (or partially tax-deductible) if you meet certain tests:

1. Neither you nor your spouse participates in a retirement plan at work. In that case, your entire IRA contribution remains deductible.
2. If you or your spouse is covered by an employer's plan, but your adjusted gross income falls below certain limits. If your income is over $50,000 for a married couple or $35,000 for a single person, you cannot deduct any portion of your IRA contribution. If your income is $40,000 or less (for marrieds) or $25,000 or less (for singles), you may deduct your entire IRA contribution.

Between those two sets of limits, the deductibility of IRA contributions gradually phases out. The formula you would use to calculate your maximum deductible contribution is explained in IRS Publication 590, "Individual Retirement Arrangement," available from the IRS at 800-TAX-FORM.

Even if you are no longer eligible for a fully or partially deductible IRA, investing in a nondeductible IRA may still make sense. For one thing, the money in your IRA will grow tax-deferred until you withdraw it. For another, money in an IRA is easier to withdraw than money in an employer-sponsored pension plan in the case of a financial emergency, though you would still be subject to taxes and possibly other penalties.

One downside to nondeductible IRAs is that you must file an extra tax form, Form 8606, to report your contribution each year. Another is that when you begin to make IRA withdrawals, you will have to prorate withdrawals between the taxable and nontaxable portions of your total IRA assets, which could become confusing. So whatever you do, be sure to keep good records of your IRA contributions and whether or not they were tax-deductible.

Investing your IRA. The law allows you to put your IRA money in a wide range of different types of investments, among them, mutual funds. Some fund companies market funds specifically for IRA accounts. Funds generally charge an annual maintenance fee on IRA accounts, typically of $10 or so per account; for that reason, it makes sense to concentrate your IRA contributions in a few good funds.

The considerations in choosing a fund for an IRA are virtually identical to those for picking funds outside of an IRA. How soon are you likely to need your money? How much risk can you afford to take with it in the meantime? Is your money properly diversified among different types of investments?

One type of fund, though, makes no sense for an IRA: a municipal bond fund. As mentioned earlier in this book, the money you withdraw from your IRA at retirement will be considered taxable income, regardless of what it was invested in. So rather than invest in municipal bonds for your IRA, you would do better to put your money in a higher-yield, though taxable, investment. Invest in municipal bonds, if you want to, outside of your tax-deferred accounts.

RETIREMENT INVESTING FOR THE SELF-EMPLOYED

If you have your own business, either full-time or as a sideline, you can save toward retirement and at the same time reduce your current tax burden. Two retirement vehicles are open to you: Keogh plans and Simplified Employee Pensions, or SEPs.

How Keogh Plans Work

Keogh plans, named for the congressman who championed the legislation that led to their creation, resemble the retirement plans offered by employers. They can be structured either as defined-contribution plans or as defined-benefit plans. If you have employees, other than your spouse, you must make contributions for them as well.

The money you invest in a Keogh plan is not taxable until you

you may want to begin tapping your existing accounts for income and to gradually reduce the risk of your overall portfolio. Consider, for example, taking some of your stock fund distributions in cash, rather than having them automatically reinvested. That approach is simpler for tax purposes than writing a check against your fund, because you won't have to go through the hassle of figuring out the cost basis for shares that you sold. You'll owe tax simply on the income you received.

You may also want to begin systematically withdrawing money from your funds. To determine how long your capital will last, you'll need to estimate what percentage of it you need to withdraw each year. You'll also need to make an educated conservative guess about the rate of return on the money that remains in your account.

Even if you're so wealthy that you won't need to tap your mutual fund accounts in retirement, you will have to (by law) begin making withdrawals from your IRAs and similar tax-deferred accounts after you reach the age of 70½.

Mutual Funds and Your Estate

You can't take them with you. But you can take steps to make sure that your mutual funds go to the heirs of your choice.

Like your other assets, your mutual funds are part of your estate. If they're jointly owned by you and another person, such as your spouse, they will pass automatically to that person when you die. Otherwise, they will be distributed according to the terms of your will, if you have one. If you die without a will, they will be distributed according to the intestacy laws of your state. State laws differ, but they will usually divide your estate among your spouse, children, and possibly other relatives, using a predetermined formula. That formula may or may not result in your assets being distributed the way you would have wished— which is one very good reason to make a will if you don't already have one.

Currently, the first $600,000 of assets in your estate (if your estate totals less than $10 million) are exempt from federal estate tax. Your state may set a lower limit before its own death taxes kick in. An unlimited marital deduction also allows you to pass any amount of wealth to your spouse, free of federal tax.

In preparing a will, you should list all the mutual funds you own and how you own them (such as individually or jointly), along with their current value. You should also write down the account numbers of each fund. If you have certificates representing ownership of fund shares, be sure to indicate where they are located (such as in a safe-deposit box).

Keeping good records—and keeping them in a place where your survivors will know to look for them—should help reduce your estate's legal fees. It will also make the work of your executor that much easier.

Mutual funds that you own in an Individual Retirement Account or Keogh plan can pass directly to a beneficiary you have designated. When you open one of these accounts, the fund company will probably ask you to name one or more primary beneficiaries. You can assign a percentage of your account's value to each of several beneficiaries, or you can leave 100 percent to one beneficiary. You may also be asked to name secondary beneficiaries in case you outlive your primary ones.

Finally, if you're called on to serve as the executor for someone's estate, and that person didn't leave behind clear fund records, you will have to do some detective work. Some places to look for clues include:

• The deceased's most recent tax return, which should list any fund holdings on Schedule B. Tax-free municipal bond funds may not be listed there, but if the deceased owned any, the tax-exempt interest income they paid should have been reported on Form 1040.

• Any brokerage firm or financial planner that the deceased did business with should have records of those accounts.

• The deceased's checkbook and canceled checks may indicate fund purchases or sales.

Also keep an eye out for any mail that arrives from fund companies. A newsletter or advertising flyer from a fund may indicate that the deceased had accounts there.

6

TAXES
AND MUTUAL FUNDS

Investing in mutual funds can greatly complicate your tax life. But it doesn't have to, if you consider the tax consequences before you make any major moves. The tax rules that affect mutual fund investors are fairly straightforward (as tax rules go).

There are basically three times in the course of your fund investing when you'll need to concern yourself with taxes:

· When you sell fund shares
· When you receive dividends or capital-gains distributions from a fund
· When you prepare your tax return for the year

WHEN YOU SELL FUND SHARES

Whenever you sell your shares in a mutual fund, you will owe tax on any profit you make. (Tax-deferred accounts are an exception here; your gains won't be taxed until you withdraw the money.) Your profit is the difference between what you paid for each share and what you sold it for. Your fund will send you a Form 1099-B early each year if you sold shares during the previous year. It will supply the same information to the IRS.

That applies to so-called tax-free funds as well. While the income you earn on such a fund is generally not subject to federal income tax (and sometimes not to state or local income taxes, either), you still must pay tax on any profit you make when you sell your shares.

You should report your mutual fund profits as capital gains on Schedule D of your tax return. A profit is considered a short-term gain if you owned the shares you sold for a year or less, a long-term gain if you owned them for more than a year.

If you sell your shares for a loss rather than for a profit, you can take some consolation in knowing that your loss may be used, in full, to offset any capital gains you had for the year. And if your capital losses exceed your capital gains, they may be used to offset up to $3,000 of ordinary income in one year. You may carry over any excess on your tax returns in following years.

Note that when you switch money from one mutual fund to another in the same fund family, that's also considered a sale, for tax purposes. As far as the IRS is concerned, you sold your shares in the old fund in order to buy your shares in the new one.

It's also considered a sale when you write a check against a fund to redeem shares, which is one argument against using your checkwriting privileges very often. Though checkwriting may be a great convenience when you need the money, every check can mean added work at tax time. This advice doesn't apply to money-market mutual funds. Because they're designed to maintain a constant share price of $1, you don't incur any capital gains or losses when you sell shares. If you're looking for a mutual fund to serve primarily as a checking account for large purchases, a money-market fund is probably your best bet.

To determine your profit or loss when you sell, you'll need to figure what's known as your "cost basis" for each share, usually what you paid for the share, which includes any commissions or load charges you paid, as well. For example, if you invested $1,000 in a no-load fund and received 45.326 shares in return, your cost basis is $22.06 per share. If you invested $1,000 in a 5-percent-load fund and received the same number of shares, your cost basis would still be $22.06 per share, even though $50 of your investment would have gone to pay the load and only $950 would have gone into your account. If your fund charges a back-end load when you sell, that load will be subtracted from the sales price of your shares (as opposed to your cost basis).

There are a number of different methods you can use to determine your cost basis:

Share identification. If you sell some, but not all, of the shares you own in a fund, you're allowed to designate which shares you are selling. Obviously, it would behoove you to sell the most expensive shares first in order to reduce your taxable profit. To do that, you must specify which shares you are selling at the time of the sale, and you must receive from the fund company or your broker a written confirmation to that effect. Investors have not always been successful in trying to obtain such confirmations, apparently because some fund companies and brokers consider it a bother. Certainly, there's no harm in trying.

Average basis. Another way that you may be able to reduce your taxable profit is by figuring an average cost basis for the shares you sell. There are two methods you can use: the double-category method and the single-category method.

With the *double-category method,* you divide your shares into two categories: long-term (for shares you've held for longer than a year) and short-term (for shares you've held a year or less). You then divide the total cost basis of all shares in each category by the number of shares in that category to determine an average basis. For example, suppose you invested $1,000 three years ago and bought 45.326 shares worth $22.06 each. Then, two years ago you invested another $1,000 and received 41.339 shares worth $24.19 each. Since all of those shares were purchased more than a year ago, they would fall into the long-term category. Their cost basis per share would be $2,000 divided by 86.665 (45.326 plus 41.339), or $23.08. You could do a similar calculation to determine the cost basis of shares in the short-term category. When you sell shares, you can specify which category (long-term or short-term) of shares you are selling. Again, you must receive written confirmation from the fund or your broker for this to work.

With the *single-category method,* you simply divide the total cost basis of all your shares by the number of shares in your account, to determine an average basis per share.

A further complication: Once you elect to use the average basis method for selling fund shares, the IRS requires that you continue to use it for your accounts at that mutual fund company unless you receive permission from the IRS to revoke it.

First in, first out. If you don't try to reduce your taxable profit by specifying which shares you're selling or by figuring an average basis for your shares, the IRS will assume that the first shares you sell are the first ones you bought. That can obviously be costly, since a fund's share price should rise over time. But it's also the simplest way of determining your cost basis because it doesn't require any special notification to the fund or to the IRS.

Whatever method you use to determine your cost basis, don't forget to include any reinvested dividends that you have already paid taxes on. For example, suppose you bought shares in a mutual fund five years ago for $1,000, received $100 in dividends each year, and had those dividends automatically reinvested in more shares. The total cost basis for your shares isn't just the original $1,000, but $1,000 plus the reinvested dividends, or $1,500.

Determining cost basis is clearly another reason why it is important to keep good records of what you pay for fund shares.

WHEN YOU RECEIVE DIVIDENDS OR CAPITAL-GAINS DISTRIBUTIONS

Any dividends or capital-gains distributions you receive from a fund (other than a tax-free fund, in the case of dividends) are considered taxable income for the year in which they are declared. That's true whether you receive them in the form of a check from your fund or have them automatically reinvested to buy more shares for your account. Note that in some instances, a fund will declare a year-end distribution that you may not receive until early the following year. That distribution is still taxable for the year it was declared, rather than the year you received it. The fund will send you and the IRS a Form 1099-DIV at the beginning of each year, showing the distributions you received during the previous year.

Tax-free funds pay income that is usually not subject to federal income tax. If the fund invests entirely in the state where you live, its income may be immune to state and local income taxes as well. Any capital-gains distributions you receive, however, may be taxable.

Other types of funds also have tax advantages. For example, some funds focus on capital growth rather than on income (see chapter 2). They may not pay dividends at all, but instead may reward you with an increase in the value of your shares. That can be an advantage if you want to put off paying taxes, because you won't owe tax on the appreciation in share price until you finally sell your shares. You will, of course, still have to pay tax on any capital-gains distributions the fund makes to you.

WHEN YOU PREPARE YOUR TAX RETURN FOR THE YEAR

The Form 1099-DIV, 1099-B, or other annual statement that each fund you own sends you will supply most of the information you need at tax time. You should report your dividends and capital-gains distributions on Schedule B of Form 1040.

If you sold fund shares during the year, you'll have to report those transactions on Schedule D, as described earlier in this chapter.

Unless you made other transactions during the year that would necessitate your filing a Schedule D, you can report any capital-gains distributions you received on your Form 1040. But, depending on your tax bracket, it may be advantageous to use Schedule D anyhow because, at this writing, it allows you to figure your gain using a maximum tax rate of 28 percent.

The Form 1099-DIV you receive may also indicate that the fund made a distribution during the year that represented a return of capital. Such distributions shouldn't be confused with capital-gains distributions. A return-of-capital distribution isn't a profit; it simply means that the fund, for one reason or another, gave you back some of your own money during the year. For that reason, a return-of-capital distribution, unlike a capital-gains distribution, isn't taxable. You do have to report it, though, on Schedule B of your tax form.

A return-of-capital distribution can also affect the cost basis of your shares, a figure you will need to know when you sell them. Suppose you bought shares in a mutual fund for $10 each. During the first year the fund made a return-of-capital distribution of $1 a share, and the next year it made a similar distribution of $2 a share. Your cost basis at that point would be $7 per share. Bear in mind that, for tax purposes, non-taxable distributions can't reduce your cost basis below zero. If they do, you must pay tax on the excess, because you will have received more money for your shares than you paid for them—in other words, a profit.

If you own shares in an international or global mutual fund, the

Form 1099-DIV you receive from your fund may have an entry in the column headed Foreign Tax Paid. That entry shows how much tax the fund paid to foreign countries on your behalf. You can get a credit for those taxes against your federal income tax by filing Form 1116, Foreign Tax Credit. Or you can report foreign taxes on Schedule A as an itemized deduction.

You stand to gain the most by claiming the credit, because that will reduce your income tax by the full amount of the foreign taxes you paid. If you claim them as a deduction, they will reduce only your taxable income. Form 1116 does require some extra effort, so it may not be worth your time if the amount of money involved is small. IRS Publication 514, "Foreign Tax Credit for Individuals," explains the rules in detail. For a copy, call 800-TAX-FORM.

You may be tempted to leave all these considerations to your accountant or tax preparer, if you use one. Even so, you'll almost certainly save on tax-preparation fees if you have all your 1099 forms and other relevant tax information ready for your tax preparer's inspection. If you discover some tax information has gotten lost in the shuffle, a quick call to your fund's 800 number will usually get you a replacement copy of whatever you need.

TAX-FREE FUNDS

Mutual funds that invest in the municipal bonds issued by state and local governments and their agencies are often referred to as tax-free funds. The dividends they pay are generally not subject to federal income tax. If the fund invests only in municipal bonds issued in your state, the dividends you earn may also be free from state and local income taxes. For that reason, single-state municipal bond funds often advertise themselves as "double" or "triple" tax-free.

Keep in mind that tax-free funds sometimes distribute capital gains to their shareholders. That happens when the fund sells securities it owns at a profit. Any capital-gains distributions you receive from a tax-free fund are subject to federal income tax and may also be subject to state and local income taxes, just as they would be if they were from a taxable fund.

Municipal bonds usually pay a lower rate of interest than taxable bonds, such as those issued by corporations, but they compensate investors through their tax advantages. Table 2.2 on page 35 shows how some taxable and nontaxable yields compare for investors in different tax brackets. The basic lesson to take away from the table is that the higher your tax bracket, the more sensible an investment a municipal bond fund may be.

In recent years the IRS has required investors with tax-exempt interest income to report that income on Form 1040. Although you may not be taxed on any municipal bond income, you'll need to save your end-of-the-year account statement from the fund as backup for your tax return.

Also keep in mind that, as mentioned earlier, any profit (or loss) you incur when you sell shares in a municipal bond fund has to be reported on Schedule D.

Investors who receive Social Security benefits should note another wrinkle in the tax code. The interest they earn from municipal bonds must be counted when they calculate the portion of their Social Security benefits (if any) that is subject to income tax. Those rules are explained in IRS Publication 915, "Social Security Benefits and Equivalent Railroad Retirement Benefits," available from the IRS at 800-TAX-FORM.

Another complication for some taxpayers is the Alternative Minimum Tax, or AMT. It generally affects taxpayers with both large incomes and large tax deductions. If you are subject to the AMT, some of your municipal bond fund interest (the part from certain bonds that are themselves subject to the AMT) may be taxable. Your fund should report to you the percentage of its income subject to the AMT for your tax calculations, if necessary. If you are not subject to the AMT yourself, your fund's AMT income needn't concern you. IRS Publication 909, "Alternative Minimum Tax for Individuals," explains the rules.

SAVING ON STATE TAXES

The interest you receive on bonds issued by the federal government is also exempt from state and local income taxes, but not from federal income taxes. This is also true for mutual funds that invest primarily in those bonds, typically referred to as government-bond funds.

Other types of mutual funds may keep only a portion of their portfolio invested in United States government securities. Depending on the tax laws of your state, you may not have to pay state income tax on that portion of your income from the fund. Your fund should supply you with the necessary information by tax time each year.

WHERE TO GET HELP

The IRS publications cited in this chapter should answer many of your tax-related questions. IRS Publication 564, "Mutual Fund Distributions," though not cited earlier, may be the most useful of all. It's revised annually, and the new edition is usually available by the end of January. For a copy of it or any other IRS publication or form, call 800-TAX-FORM.

An accountant or tax preparer should be able to help you, too—for a fee, of course. But don't overlook one often useful source of free guidance on tax matters: your fund itself. Many funds can field basic tax questions on their toll-free 800 numbers.

Note also that in recent years Congress has discussed adopting new rules that would require fund companies to provide cost-basis information to investors who have sold shares. No law has been enacted as of this writing, though some funds have begun to provide the information voluntarily as a service to their shareholders.

Simple Record Keeping for Tax Purposes

You can't always count on a mutual fund to generate profits, but in good times or bad you can count on it to generate paperwork. As an investor you may receive monthly account statements from each fund your own, plus prospectuses, annual and semiannual reports, newsletters, and announcements of new funds from that fund company. Pretty soon, you may feel overwhelmed by it all. You may even find yourself approaching your mailbox with a sense of dread.

Fortunately, you don't have to keep all that paper. You don't even have to save very much of it, unless you want to. The only papers you absolutely must save are those relating to your taxes. (And even those can probably be replaced by the fund, usually for a modest fee, if you should lose them.)

As a general rule, you should save enough of your account statements to establish the cost basis for the fund shares you have bought. Remember, you'll need that when you eventually sell those shares.

You should also save the Form 1099-DIV or other annual statement that you receive from each fund after the end of the tax year. Those can be important if your tax return is challenged by the IRS.

You needn't save them forever, though. The IRS usually has three years from the annual tax return filing deadline to challenge your return. For most people, that deadline is April 15. So, for example, if your 1994 tax return is due by April 15, 1995, the IRS would have until April 15, 1998, to complete an audit of that return. If you haven't heard from the IRS by then, you could presumably throw out the fund records you used in preparing that return.

You'd be wise, however, to hang on to them a bit longer. For one thing, there are exceptions to the three-year guideline. If the IRS suspects that you underreported your income by a significant amount, it can generally audit your return as late as six years after the filing deadline. And if you're suspected of fraud, the IRS can come after you at any time in the future. So if you have the space, you may want to keep your tax records forever.

Forever is not the appropriate time span for other mail you receive from your funds, fortunately. Most of it can be read and discarded, or discarded unread. Do take a look at the newsletters, booklets, and other educational materials your fund will send you from time to time. They often offer useful advice and may alert you to new developments, such as changes in the tax rules.

7 WHEN AND HOW TO SELL FUND SHARES

If this book has any bias at all, it is biased toward buying shares in good mutual funds and holding on to them for a long time. We believe that is the best way for most people to invest their money. The readers of *Consumer Reports* appear to heed that advice. A survey of readers who invest in mutual funds found that 94 percent hold their funds for the long term.

However, the day may come when, for one reason or another, you'll want to sell some of your fund shares. You may need the money for a down payment on a new home or to pay a college tuition bill. You may be dissatisfied with a fund's performance or have decided to change the makeup of your personal fund portfolio.

Before you decide to sell your fund shares, always take a look at the alternatives. There could be good reasons for keeping your funds if you can sell something else. It may even make sense under some circumstances to borrow money instead. For example, if you're saving toward a distant goal, such as retirement, cashing in your fund shares for a more immediate need, such as paying a large bill, will certainly slow your progress. It may take months or years to build your fund accounts back to their present level.

Selling a fund also has tax ramifications. If you bought your fund shares years ago and have seen them rise steadily in value ever since, you may owe a large capital-gains tax when you sell. Even if your fund didn't make a lot of money, selling it will introduce more tax complications into your life than, for example, cashing in a bank CD. You will need to determine the cost basis (that is, the price you paid) for the fund shares you sell. That can be tricky if you bought shares at different times (see chapter 6).

The bottom line is, if you have investments other than mutual funds, consider selling those first.

SELL SIGNALS

Aside from the purely personal reasons that might make you consider selling a fund, funds themselves undergo changes that may make you want to consider selling. Here are a few of them.

The Fund's Manager Changes

If the man or woman or team that led your fund to past glory is replaced (and you hear about it), you may wonder whether to sell. That's a tough call. Often new managers don't do as well as their predecessors, especially in the first year or two. Other times, a new manager will outperform the old one right from the start. Our advice in most instances: Give the new manager a chance, but keep a closer eye than usual on your fund's performance relative to other funds of its type. If after a reasonable period of time, say two years, the fund hasn't done as well as you think it would have under the old regime, consider shopping for a new fund with similar investment objectives.

The Fund Changes Its Objectives

Sometimes fund companies will take an existing fund and give it a new mission. Perhaps the fund has been a poor performer, or perhaps the fund company sees an unfilled marketing niche and doesn't want to go to the trouble of launching a new fund to take advantage of it. The fund may also get a new name in the process. If that happens to a fund you own, the question you need to ask yourself is whether the fund's new objectives are still in keeping with your personal objectives. If not, start shopping for a new fund right away. Remember, there are plenty of funds to choose from.

The Fund's Fees Change

If your fund switches from being a no-load fund to a load fund (that is, it begins imposing sales charges whenever you buy shares), think about selling. These days, such a metamorphosis is most likely to occur when a fund that had eliminated its load for a limited period of time in order to attract new investors reinstates that load. Of course, if you don't plan to buy more shares and are otherwise satisfied with that fund's performance, there is no reason to sell.

By the same token, don't rush to sell a load fund you already own just because this book (or some other book) has convinced you that you should invest only in no-loads. Since you have already paid the load, and can't get it back, you may as well keep the fund, as long as it is performing up to your expectations.

Also keep an eye on other fees your fund charges. If its management expenses rise year after year (you can sometimes tell from the prospectus) or if it imposes new fees on shareholders, consider switching to a fund that's better at keeping its costs in check.

SELLING IN STAGES

Selling mutual fund shares is relatively easy, which is one of the reasons people buy funds in the first place. Depending on how you set up your account when you opened it, you may be able to sell fund shares simply by phoning the fund. The proceeds can be sent to you in the form of a check or deposited directly into your bank account.

At some funds, you may have to fill out a redemption request and obtain a signature guarantee. Obtaining a signature guarantee is much like having a document notarized: A bank officer or brokerage firm representative will have to authenticate your signature. This procedure can obviously be a nuisance if you need your money in a hurry. But, in any case, the fund will buy your shares back from you. You won't have to find a buyer for them, as you would with some other types of investments.

If you don't need a large amount of money all at once, but have the luxury of redeeming your fund shares in stages, you can try a strategy called "averaging out." For example, if you need the money to pay for home improvements, you can redeem just enough shares at each stage to pay your bills as they come due. You could also try it if you need a lump sum at a certain future date, such as a down payment on a house; simply redeem blocks of shares each week or month and deposit the money in a bank or money-market account until you have enough set aside.

Averaging out is the mirror image of the buying strategy called dollar-cost averaging discussed in chapter 3. You redeem a set number of shares every week, month, or whatever time period suits you. That way you reduce your risk of taking all your money out on a day when share prices are unusually low.

In some cases, you might want to begin averaging out as much as a year or two ahead of the time you expect to need the money. For example, if the stock market is at a record high level and your entire college tuition stake is tied up in an aggressive-growth stock fund, it may make sense to begin slowly selling shares and putting the money in a fund with little likelihood of losing money. A money-market fund or a short-term bond fund, for example, would make sense for that purpose. Similarly, as you near retirement, you may want to average out of some of your more aggressive funds.

SELLING AND TAXES

The basic tax rules that mutual fund investors need to concern themselves with are explained in chapter 6. Many of those rules come into effect when you sell shares.

When you contemplate selling, remember that there are several ways to determine the cost basis (your original price) for the shares you sell. It may, for example, be of benefit to you to instruct your fund to sell the shares you bought on a specific date. So be sure to examine the tax rules before you make any moves. Also bear in mind that if you owe a substantial amount of tax on the shares you sell, you'll have to come up with that money by the time you file your next tax return. Therefore, you may want to put a portion of your profits aside for next year's taxes.

SELL OR SWITCH?

Selling a fund doesn't necessarily mean leaving that fund's family. Many fund companies offer a wide range of different types of funds (see chapter 8). If, say, you need to pay college tuition bills, you could switch money from a stock fund into a money-market fund at that same fund company, usually with just a phone call. You could then pay those bills with checks drawn against the money-market fund.

But keep in mind that switching money from one fund to another is a taxable event in the eyes of the IRS. That is, you are seen as having sold one fund and bought another, even though your money probably never left the same building. So you could owe income taxes on any capital gains you made on the first fund, just as if you had taken your profits in cash.

Still, the ability to move money from fund to fund with just a phone call is one of the great advantages of mutual fund investing. Funds differ in their rules about how often you can switch, so it's worth calling their toll-free numbers to inquire about the rules before you make any moves. Also be sure to ask whether you'll incur any loads (or sales charges) on the funds you buy or any redemption fees (or deferred sales charges) on the ones you sell. Such charges can eat away at your investment dollars, particularly if you switch more often than absolutely necessary.

REBALANCING YOUR PORTFOLIO

If you are following an asset-allocation strategy, such as those outlined in chapter 4, you may need to rebalance your portfolio from time to time. Rebalancing is necessary when one of your investments outgrows the percentage you allotted for it in your asset-allocation plan.

For example, suppose you decided to put 10 percent of your money in an international stock fund and 20 percent in a U.S. growth stock fund, as part of a diversified portfolio of four or five funds. If foreign stock markets boom and the U.S. stock market drops in value, you may find yourself with 15 percent of your money in the international stock fund and just 17 percent in the growth stock fund. To get your portfolio back in sync, you could sell enough of your international stock fund shares to shrink it back down to 10 percent of your portfolio and use the proceeds to buy enough new shares in your growth stock fund to bring it back up to 20 percent. If the two funds are part of the same fund family, you could accomplish that simply by switching.

An even better strategy, if you have the money, would be to leave your international fund as is and add enough money to your growth stock fund and the others in your portfolio to return them all to their original percentages. That way, you'll have more money invested in your fund accounts, and you won't miss out if international funds, for example, continue their boom.

WHEN NOT TO SELL

There are good reasons to sell a mutual fund, and there are bad reasons. One bad reason is because a fund salesperson tells you that your money will be better off in Fund Y than in Fund X (which that same salesperson may have sold you earlier). The salesperson may be honestly looking after your best interests or may simply want to earn a commission from the fund you'd be moving into. If you're satisfied with the performance of the fund you already own, don't be too easily persuaded to switch. Be particularly skeptical of predictions of great future performance by the new fund. The salesperson couldn't possibly know. Nobody knows.

Another bad reason to sell is because the stock market is falling and your fund is falling along with it. Markets fall from time to time; funds do, too. That doesn't mean that your fund is not well managed or that it won't rise again when the market comes back. (If the market keeps rising and your fund keeps falling, that's another matter. And it's probably a good reason to sell.) Unless you need that money immediately to pay your bills, try to ride out any market declines. Far too many investors bail out during downturns and come back only when the market is booming once more. Their sell-low, buy-high strategy practically guarantees poor investment results.

Likewise, don't panic in a crash. When the stock market crashed in October 1987, the S&P 500 market index lost 24 percent of its value in just a few days. Countless mutual fund investors panicked and sold; many vowed that they'd never risk their money in the stock market again.

While those investors sat on the sidelines, the S&P 500 gained 16.5 percent in 1988 and another 31.7 percent in 1989. Though it's always possible that some future stock market crash will make the crash of '87 seem like a mere blip on the charts, its lesson is worth bearing in mind. Investors who sold in a panic lost money. Investors who kept their fund shares eventually made money. And investors with the luck or savvy to buy right after the crash made even more money.

8 GETTING GOOD SERVICE FROM YOUR FUND

Companies that manage more than one mutual fund often refer to themselves as a "fund family." For advertising purposes, that's certainly more appealing than "big impersonal financial institution."

Advertising considerations aside, there are certain advantages to investing in several funds in the same fund family (or families) rather than separate funds spread across different families. One is that some fund companies offer financial incentives. For example, a fund company that normally charges a $10-per-account maintenance fee for IRAs may cap its total fees at, say, $30; if you have four IRAs, all in different funds but at the same fund company, you'll escape paying a maintenance fee every year on that fourth IRA.

BEFORE YOU INVEST

Probably more important to most investors, though, is the convenience that investing in a family of funds offers. So when you shop for a mutual fund, it's wise to make sure that both a given fund and its parent company are good fits for you.

First, make sure the family offers a wide enough variety of funds to meet your current and future investing needs, to the extent that you can predict them. Fund families may have just a handful of funds for you to choose from, or they may offer more than 100. Fidelity Investments, the most prolific spawner of new funds, has well over 200 funds in its family. You may not need a family that offers dozens of specialized or exotic funds, but you'll probably do best with one that offers at least a selection of stock and bond funds of different types and a money-market fund.

Along with the size of a fund family, consider service. Though service doesn't get as much press attention as performance (probably because performance is much easier to quantify), it will be a major factor in how satisfied you are with your fund investments in the years ahead. Your goal should be to buy mutual funds that deliver both good performance and good service.

All else being equal, go with the fund whose family offers the package of individual services that you're most likely to use. Here are some of the important services to consider.

Telephone Switching

At some point in the future, you may want to move money out of one mutual fund and into another fund. Perhaps you're unhappy with the performance of the fund you own or perhaps your goals have changed, making that fund now inappropriate for you. At many fund families you can switch your money to any fund in that family with just a phone call.

You may have to sign up for that service when opening your account. Otherwise, the fund will accept only written instructions from you, and it may require a signature guarantee from a bank or brokerage firm. Obtaining a signature guarantee can be a time-consuming and aggravating process, especially if you need your money in a hurry. Even if you don't sign up for switching when you first apply, you can usually have the service added to your account later on.

When inquiring about telephone switching, you may want to ask whether the fund family charges new sales loads when you switch from one load fund to another. At some fund families, once you've paid a load to buy shares, you can redeem those shares to buy shares in another load fund without incurring a second load. Our advice, of course, is to avoid buying load funds in the first place.

You may also want to ask the fund if it limits you to a certain number of switches per year without penalty. Some families now impose such limits, primarily as a way to discourage short-term investors who switch from fund to fund in pursuit of quick profits. For investors who buy good mutual funds and hold them for the long term, restrictions on how often you may switch should be irrelevant. But if you're tempted to speculate, keep them in mind.

Finally, find out what hours your fund's telephone lines are open for you to make transactions. Some are open only during normal business hours; if you call after that, you may at least be able to check on account balances and share prices using the automated phone system. At other funds, you can reach someone 24 hours a day. That may be important to you if you work odd hours or can't easily call your fund during the day.

Checkwriting

You may want to be able to write checks to redeem your mutual fund shares periodically, in order to save yourself the trouble of withdrawing money from your fund, depositing it in your checking account at the bank, and then writing a check. Some types of funds, primarily bond funds, offer checkwriting and will provide a pad of checks when your account is opened. There may be a limit to the number of checks you can write per month or year, and the checks may have to be written for at least a certain minimum amount, such as $250 or $500.

Even if a fund whose shares you'd like to buy won't allow checkwriting against your balance, you can still gain the convenience of checkwriting by opening a money-market fund account at the same fund family. Then you can switch money from, say, your stock fund into the money-market fund and write a check. Money-market mutual funds typically pay a higher rate of interest than interest-bearing checking accounts at banks, even the ones that call themselves "money-market" accounts. Money-market mutual funds are not, however, federally insured.

Bear in mind that when you write a check against a mutual fund, you are really selling some of your shares back to the fund. For any type of mutual fund but a money-market fund, that will usually mean a capital gain or a capital loss, depending on how much money you received for the shares you sold and how much you paid for them originally. (Money-market funds aren't affected, because they maintain a stable share price of $1.) Accordingly, every check you write can further complicate your tax return for the year (see chapter 7).

Linking Your Funds to Your Bank

Another way to move money from a mutual fund account to a bank account is called a wire transfer or electronic funds transfer. It allows you to tell the fund company to redeem shares and put the money in your bank account. Typically, you'll need to supply your fund company with a voided personal check from your bank in order to set up this service.

You may also be able to arrange for money to move in the other direction—from your bank account to your fund account. For example, you may instruct the fund to automatically take a certain amount of money each month from your bank account and buy fund shares for you. That's a virtually effortless way to set up a regular investment program. It also allows you to enjoy the benefits of dollar-cost averaging, an investing technique explained in chapter 3.

Some funds will even waive their minimum initial investment requirements if you sign up for a series of regular investments through your bank account. That sort of arrangement can help you get started in fund investing if you can't commit $1,000 or $2,000 up front.

The Subjective Aspects of Service

Compared to many other industries, the mutual fund industry has a pretty good record of continuously upgrading its customer service. Fund companies' automated telephone systems are better than they were some years ago, their account statements are easier to read, and their prospectuses are inching toward comprehensibility. At least part of the reason is that the mutual fund trade is intensely competitive and fund investors are, by and large, knowledgeable consumers who can easily take their business elsewhere if they're displeased.

Fund families, like human families, differ in style. You may not be able to perfectly predict whether you'll be happy in a given family unless you've actually tried it. But you can get a glimpse of what's in store for you if you pay attention to the following clues early on.

1. The phones. When you phone for the prospectus of a fund you're interested in buying, are you able to get through to a service representative reasonably quickly? Reconsider your plans if all you get is a busy signal or if you find yourself on hold for a half hour, listening to "Do You Know the Way to San Jose?" over and over again. A fund that's difficult to reach when you want to buy shares may be all the more unreachable when you need to sell them.

A *Consumer Reports* survey of readers who owned mutual funds found that being unable to reach their funds by phone when they wanted to ranked high on those readers' lists of irritations. More than 9 percent of our survey respondents complained that telephone assistance was not available when they wanted it, and nearly the same percentage complained of busy signals or lengthy holds. That survey was published in 1990, and many fund companies have upgraded their phone systems since then. But the number of people investing in funds has also increased, further burdening the phone lines. Test the phone service to see if you can get through when you want to.

2. The people. When you reach a service representative, is that person pleasant and helpful? More to the point, is he or she able to answer your questions or at least transfer you to someone who can? Service reps are, in essence, the face that a fund company shows its public. If a service rep comes across like a buffoon, imagine what sort of people may work behind the scenes at that fund. In the survey cited above, just over 9 percent of readers complained of fund representatives who were not helpful or not knowledgeable.

3. The paper. When you receive the information you requested from the fund (if it takes a long time or if you never receive anything, that's a clue in itself), look it over carefully. Is it clearly written and understandable to the average investor? Does it answer your questions forthrightly or bury key information in fine print? Are the forms you would need to fill out understandable?

You may also want to ask a fund representative to describe the fund's account statements—the most important paperwork you will receive after you buy shares in that fund family. Some fund companies issue one consolidated statement for all the funds you own in that family; others send separate statements for each fund. Consolidated statements will make your record keeping easier and reduce the number of papers you have to save. You'll find, as a fund investor, that paper piles up quickly, and you will need to save some of it for future tax purposes.

Fund paperwork was the single greatest source of dissatisfaction in *Consumer Reports'* survey of fund investors. More than 15 percent complained of excessive mailings. Nearly 11 percent complained of unclear account statements—though, interestingly, fewer than 4 percent said their account statements were inaccurate. However well managed they are in other respects, some funds clearly have trouble in the communications department.

These clues to fund service are not as superficial as they might seem. Investing in a mutual fund involves at least a few phone calls and a lot of paperwork—when you first sign up, when you later buy or sell shares, at tax time each year, and on other occasions. A fund that knows how to communicate effectively, by phone and on paper, will do far less to complicate your life than a fund that doesn't. And simplifying things, of course, is one of the reasons you may have decided to invest in mutual funds in the first place.

AFTER YOU INVEST

You can improve your odds of getting good fund service if you choose funds with service in mind and if you sign up for all the optional services you're likely to need when you first open your account. In many cases, you can add those services later on, but that requires more work on your part.

Once you're a shareholder in a fund, is there anything you can do to improve the service you receive? Absolutely. Here are a few time and aggravation savers.

First, get to know your fund family's phone system. Most are highly automated and will allow you to check your account balances and conduct all sorts of transactions simply by pushing a few buttons on your phone. (If you don't already have a push-button phone, you may want to invest in one.) Your fund should be able to provide you with a booklet or other information on how to use its phone system.

TABLE 8.1   THE BIGGEST FUND FAMILIES

Table 8.1 includes the 30 largest mutual fund families and their total assets as of August 1993. Companies whose toll-free phone numbers are shown in the column at right sell shares directly to the public; the rest sell primarily through local representatives. For the toll-free numbers of other fund companies, call directory assistance, 800-555-1212. TTY numbers are for teletypewriters, sometimes referred to as Telecommunications Devices for the Deaf, or TDDs.

NAME	TOTAL ASSETS (BILLIONS)	PHONE (800-)
Fidelity Investments	$215.6	544-8888
		TTY: 544-0118
The Vanguard Group	124.3	662-7447
		TTY: 662-2738
Merrill Lynch Asset Management	113.3	—
Capital Research and Management	92.7	—
Franklin Group/Templeton	86.0	—
The Dreyfus Corporation	76.5	645-6561
		TTY: 227-1341
Federated Investors	66.7	—
Dean Witter InterCapital	57.2	—
Putnam Funds	53.5	—
Prudential Mutual Funds	50.1	—
Kemper	46.1	—
Smith Barney Shearson	45.8	—
IDS Mutual Fund Group	41.0	—
T. Rowe Price	32.3	638-5660
		TTY: 637-0763
Scudder	32.2	225-2470
		TTY: 543-7916
SEI Financial Services	31.6	—
Oppenheimer/Centennial	24.3	—
Massachusetts Financial Services	24.2	—
Twentieth Century	23.1	345-2021
		TTY: 634-4113
AIM Group	23.0	—
Goldman Sachs & Co.	22.5	—
PaineWebber	22.3	—
Alliance Capital Management	21.5	—
Concord Financial Group	19.3	—
PNC Financial Services Group	18.5	—
Janus Funds	16.3	525-8983
		TTY: 624-5906
American Capital	15.9	—
SchwabFunds	14.1	—
The Colonial Group	13.5	—
USAA	13.1	382-8722
		TTY: 531-4327

Sources: Investment Company Institute, Washington, D.C., and the fund companies themselves

To reach a service representative by phone with the least delay, take note of the days and times you've had trouble (or no trouble) getting through. Some hours are traditionally busy for fund companies. Monday at noon, for example, is often a peak period because that's the first opportunity each week for investors to call on their lunch hours. Your fund company may be hard to reach at that time, or it may put on extra operators to handle the added volume and be even easier to reach. For an idea of the volume of calls a fund must handle, consider that Fidelity Investments, the largest fund family, receives some 200,000 customer calls on a typical day. Of those, 70,000 to 80,000 are handled by Fidelity representatives, the rest by Fidelity's automated phone system. You'll learn through experience when it's easiest to get through to your fund.

When you phone, have your account numbers handy. You'll need them to use the automated phone systems. The fund's service reps may also ask for them, depending on the nature of your request.

Don't expect much in the way of advice. The service reps who answer the phones at fund companies usually don't have the training or the credentials required to dispense investment advice. They can't tell you which funds to buy or when to sell, but they may be able to give you some general information on what types of funds are appropriate for what purposes.

Carefully check the account statements you receive from a fund, especially during the first few months. Make certain your deposits are accurately recorded. You may also want to check the share price the fund charged you for your shares against the price for that day as reported in your daily newspaper. Also make sure that any IRA contributions you make (if any) are credited toward the proper tax year. If you find the fund has made a mistake, call as soon as possible to have it corrected.

Finally, don't hesitate to move your money to another fund company if, after a reasonable trial period, you're unhappy with the service you receive. There are many good fund companies to choose from, so there's no reason to put up with a bad one.

Resolving a Dispute with Your Fund

There is no single, all-powerful agency ready to come to your aid if you have a problem involving a mutual fund. If you do find yourself in a dispute, your first course of action should be to try to work it out with the fund, the salesperson, or the salesperson's superiors. If that fails, there are a number of agencies you can turn to for assistance.

The Securities and Exchange Commission (SEC) is the federal agency whose job it is to regulate the securities industry, including mutual funds. The SEC rarely gets involved in individual cases but may be interested if your problem turns out to be part of a larger pattern of abuse. Write to:

Office of Consumer Affairs
Securities and Exchange Commission
450 Fifth Street, N.W.
Washington, DC 20549-2006

The National Association of Securities Dealers (NASD) is an industry-sponsored "self-regulatory" body overseen by the SEC. Almost all brokerage firms that do business with the public are members of the NASD. Among other things, the NASD is responsible for regulating its members' activities in the area of mutual funds. That includes investigating and arbitrating disputes with investors who bought fund shares through a broker. The NASD has 14 district offices across the United States. Its main office is in Washington, D.C. If you can't locate a district office near you, contact the main office for guidance:

National Association of Securities Dealers, Inc.
1735 K Street, N.W.
Washington, DC 20006-1506
202-728-8000

State agencies. All 50 states (as well as Washington, D.C., and the Commonwealth of Puerto Rico) have securities commissions or divisions. These offices go by a number of different names and often are divisions of other agencies, such as the state's commerce department or attorney general's office. You'll generally find them headquartered in the state capital.

States also have banking departments, which may be of assistance if the problem you have involves a fund purchased at a bank. Depending on how that bank is chartered, however, the state banking department may not have authority over it. If this is the case, contact a federal agency. The state banking department should at least be able to steer you in the right direction.

9 CONSUMER REPORTS RATINGS OF MUTUAL FUNDS

An abundance of information about the performance of mutual funds is available today in magazines, newspapers, and investment newsletters. Some might say an overabundance.

Consumer Reports adds to that abundance every few years when we publish our own Ratings of mutual funds. In addition to *Consumer Reports,* publications that rate mutual funds on a regular basis include (in alphabetical order): *Barron's, Business Week, Forbes, Fortune, Kiplinger's Personal Finance, Money, USA Today, U.S. News & World Report,* and the *Wall Street Journal.*

WHY RATINGS DIFFER

If you ever read two different publications' fund-performance tables alongside one another, you'll probably find that their figures differ somewhat. There can be many reasons for that, aside from the most obvious one: human error.

Publications often examine different time periods. In order to beat its competitors to the newsstand, for example, one magazine may base its year-end performance ratings on a year that ended earlier in December. It will show different numbers when compared to magazines that waited until after December 31 to compile their year-end performance data.

Publications also compute their data differently. For example, most ignore the effect of loads in performance. (*Consumer Reports* is an exception.)

Some publications compare their funds in terms of how investments of a certain number of dollars would have grown over a certain period of time; other publications deal solely in percentages. Those that use percentages may "annualize" them, that is, show what the fund returned, on average, for each year of a certain period of time. Or they may simply report the total percentage gain from the beginning to the end of the time period.

Publications that attempt to judge how risky funds may be also use different methods, symbols, and even definitions of what risk actually is. And when it comes to deciding how to rank funds or assign them overall scores, publications use any number of different schemes. Therefore, don't be surprised if one magazine's top-ranked fund is another magazine's middle-of-the-packer, even if both publications use basically the same data.

HOW TO READ RATINGS

When you read our Ratings or those of another publication, there are a number of questions you should ask. Generally, you'll find the answers somewhere in the fine print.

What time period did the publication look at? You probably don't want to give as much credence to performance ratings for the most recent three-month period as to ratings that are based on consistent long-term performance. Almost any fund, however well or badly managed, can have a three-month lucky or unlucky streak.

Do the performance figures or dollar accumulations reflect loads and other expenses that the funds charge? They should, because if you buy that fund you'll have to pay those charges.

What types of funds have been grouped together? It probably isn't fair to compare, for example, a balanced fund with an aggressive-growth fund. The former is supposed to be cautious by nature; the latter is far bolder. In a boom year for stocks, the balanced fund may make a respectable gain; the aggressive fund may make a spectacular one. In a tough year, the balanced fund may have a modest gain or a modest loss; the aggressive fund may suffer a dramatic decline. Depending on the time period the publication is examining, either of those funds could appear to be far superior to the other when, in fact, they may both be good or bad examples of their kind.

Also be cautious of ratings that split up the fund universe too finely. A fund that ranks first in a category with only a handful of competitors may, in fact, be mediocre when compared with all the funds that share its same basic investment objective.

Does the publication attempt to judge how risky a particular fund is? And, if so, how does it define risk? Performance data, particularly if it covers only a brief span of time, can be deceiving. A risk rating can try to show the risks a fund took on its way to that performance percentage; it can also try to predict how that fund might do under more adverse conditions. Risk should also figure in your evaluations of mutual funds. Given two funds with similar performance scores over time, you'll almost certainly do better with the one that takes fewer risks; at least you'll spend less time worrying about it.

HOW CONSUMER REPORTS RATES FUNDS

Unlike many of the products that are rated in the pages of *Consumer Reports* each month, mutual funds can be evaluated solely on their past performance. We can't take them apart in a laboratory or drive them around a test track and tell you, for sure, how they'll do tomorrow. We believe, however, that a fund with a consistently good record over time might reasonably be expected to perform better than a fund with a poor or spotty record. Indeed, when we looked in 1993 at funds that we had highly rated in 1990, we found that they had continued to perform considerably better than average as a group. Our 20 highest-rated stock funds returned an average of nearly 12 percent annually in 1991 and 1992, compared with a 10.8 percent return on the S&P 500. Our top-rated bond funds from 1990 also outperformed the average for their categories.

The performance figures in the Ratings that follow were collected for *Consumer Reports* by Morningstar, Inc., an independent fund-data vendor. Investors can contact Morningstar, Inc., by writing to them at 53 West Jackson Boulevard, Chicago, IL 60604, or calling them at 312-427-1985. The selection of funds and the methodology for determining the Ratings order were based on our judgments.

We rated 316 stock funds and 152 bond funds. In keeping with our emphasis on long-term performance, we included only funds that had been in existence for at least five years at the time of our study. We didn't rate certain types of funds, such as stock sector funds, which are generally more speculative than more diversified mutual funds. We also omitted funds that are not sold to the general public and funds that require minimum initial investments of more than $5,000.

To judge the performance of funds, we made a series of hypothetical investments: $2,000 each year for five years, for a total of $10,000. We deducted any front-end loads or sales charges from each $2,000 investment, just as the fund company would in real life. To account for redemption fees, we hypothetically "sold" the fund at the end of five years and deducted any such fees the fund would impose.

We didn't deduct the deferred sales charges that some funds impose on a sliding scale when you sell your shares. Such funds may subtract 5 percent on any shares you sell within a year of buying them, 4 percent on shares held longer than a year but less than two years, and so on. We recommend avoiding such funds if there's any possibility that you may need to take your money out within a few years. Funds with deferred sales charges are footnoted in the Ratings.

The Ratings order for both stock and bond funds is based on performance and risk. We determined risk differently for stock funds and bond funds, as explained in the introductory material that precedes each set of Ratings. We also weighted risk differently in determining final scores for each fund. Risk was given more weight in the case of bond funds because we believe that bond-fund investors are, in general, less eager to take a risk with their money.

For both sets of Ratings, we have divided the funds into categories based on their investment objectives. The stock-fund categories are listed in roughly ascending order of risk. (For more detailed explanations of the different categories, see chapter 2.)

RATINGS OF STOCK MUTUAL FUNDS

Listed in groups according to investment objective, as determined by Morningstar, Inc., the independent fund-data supplier that provided our performance figures. Within groups, listed in order of overall score. The entry in each group designated by a ▲ shows, for comparison purposes, how the S&P 500 stock market index would have scored for the five years under study.
Score. Based on five-year accumulations and risk ratings, with accumulation worth about two-thirds of the score and risk about one-third.
5 Years. How much an investor would have accumulated by investing $2,000 in the fund at the beginning of each year, 1988 through 1992. Any front-end loads (sales charges) are deducted from each investment. Any redemption fees are deducted at the end of the five-year period. Management and 12b-1

fees are also accounted for in the final dollar figure.
Risk. We compared each fund's performance with that of the S&P 500 during two periods of market decline: the stock market crash of 1987 and the bear market of June 1990 to October 1990. Funds whose performance was similar to the S&P 500 (plus or minus 20 percent) earned a ○ for that period. A fund that performed 21 to 40 percent better earned a ◐. Funds that performed more than 40 percent better got the top score,● Funds that did 21 to 40 percent worse got a ◑; funds that performed more than 40 percent worse got a ●. International funds were rated by the same method but against the Morgan Stanley World Index and with only one risk period.
Yearly performance. The fund's total returns for each year. Percentages are

rounded and do not reflect front- or back-end loads, if any. NA indicates fund was merged into another fund in 1993.
Load. Shows the front-end load, if any, each fund imposes, as of 1993 study. Redemption fees, deferred sales charges, and 12b-1 fees are footnoted. All else being equal, choose a fund with the lowest combination of loads and other fees.
Expense. The percentage of your investment that will be subtracted each year to pay the fund's operating expenses, as of 1993 study. The average for all domestic stock funds is about 1.5 percent. International stock funds average about 1.8 percent.
Minimum. The minimum investment required to open an account. Later investments and IRA contributions may be much smaller.
Phone. Number to call for a prospectus, application, or other information.

As published in *Consumer Reports*, May 1993, and updated in January 1994.

BALANCED

Fund name	Score				5 years	Risk		Yearly performance						Load	Expense	Minimum	Phone
	0	25	50	75	100	'87	'90	'89	'90	'91	'92	'93					800-
CGM Mutual					$15,600	◐○	◐●	22%	1%	41%	6%	22%	—	0.93%	$2500	345-4048
Fidelity Balanced					14,650	●●	●●	19	0	27	8	19	—	0.96	2500	544-8888

Fund	Rating	Value	—	—	—	—	—	Sales charge	Expense	Min.	Phone
MainStay Total Return	◐	15,001	15	5	37	4	11	— [1][2]	2.00	500	522-4202
Kemper Investment Total Return	◐	15,628	20	0	42	4	8	— [1][2]	2.03	250	621-1048
Pax World	●	14,222	25	11	21	1	−1	— [1]	1.10	250	767-1729
Dodge & Cox Balanced	◐	14,589	23	1	21	11	16	—	0.65	2500	[3]
▲ S&P 500	○	15,440	32	−3	31	8	10	—	—	—	—
Fidelity Advisor Income & Growth	○	15,065	25	−3	34	9	20	4.75% [1]	1.60	2500	522-7297
Fidelity Puritan	○	14,916	20	−6	24	15	21	—	0.64	2500	544-8888
Vanguard STAR	○	14,477	19	−4	24	10	11	—	NA	500	662-7447
Phoenix Balanced	◐	14,308	25	7	26	7	6	4.75 [1]	1.02	500	243-4361
Vanguard/Wellington	●	14,239	22	−3	24	8	14	—	0.37	3000	662-7447
Phoenix Income & Growth A	●	14,202	21	−2	23	13	15	5.75 [1]	1.38	250	243-4361
Strong Investment	●	12,978	11	3	20	3	15	—	1.20	250	368-1030
Kemper Total Return	○	14,511	20	4	40	2	12	5.75	1.03	1000	621-1048
MFS Total Return	○	13,726	23	−2	22	10	15	4.75 [1]	0.84	1000	225-2606
IDS Mutual	◐	13,555	19	−3	24	10	14	5.00	0.78	2000	328-8300
Keystone Custodian K-1	◐	13,544	20	−2	24	3	10	— [1][2]	1.97	1000	343-2898
American Balanced	◐	13,723	22	−2	25	9	11	5.75 [1]	0.82	500	421-0180
EV Traditional Investors	◐	13,293	21	1	21	6	11	4.75 [1]	0.91	1000	225-6265
Delaware	○	14,333	26	0	21	13	9	5.75 [1]	0.74	250	523-4640
Calvert Social Invest. Mgd. Growth	◐	13,050	19	2	18	7	6	4.75 [1]	1.28	1000	368-2748
Merrill Lynch Bal. for Invest. B	◐	13,207	17	−3	25	3	15	— [1][2]	1.89	1000	637-3863
George Putnam Fund of Boston A	◐	13,501	24	−1	23	8	11	5.75 [1]	1.06	500	225-1581
USAA Investment Cornerstone	◐	12,548	22	−9	16	6	24	—	1.18	1000	382-8722
United Continental Income	○	13,224	24	−6	26	10	13	8.50	0.80	500	366-5465

1 12b-1 fee   2 Deferred sales charge   3 415-434-0311   4 Closed to new investors at time of study.   5 414-272-6133   6 212-245-4500   7 Redemption fee if you sell within one year   8 314-727-5305   9 Redemption fee when you sell.

Data source: Morningstar, Inc.

EQUITY-INCOME

Fund name	Score (0–100)	5 years	Risk '87	Risk '90	'89	'90	'91	'92	'93	Load	Expense	Minimum	Phone 800-
Invesco Industrial Income		$16,423			32%	1%	46%	1%	17%	— [1]	0.98%	$250	525-8085
USAA Mutual Income Stock		15,156			27	-1	27	8	12	—	0.74	1000	382-8722
Smith Barney Shearson T.R. B		15,973			17	2	29	13	11	— [1][2]	1.69	1000	451-2010
SteinRoe Total Return		14,576			20	-2	30	8	12	—	0.85	1000	338-2550
Dean Witter Equity-Income		15,361			21	2	24	13	-4	— [1][2]	2.04	1000	869-3863
▲ S&P 500		$15,440			32%	-3%	31%	8%	10%	—	—	—	—
Capital Income Builder		14,288			20	4	26	10	15	5.75% [1]	0.98%	$1000	421-9900
T. Rowe Price Equity-Income		14,711			14	-7	25	14	15	—	1.05	2500	638-5660
Fidelity Equity-Income		14,259			19	-14	29	15	21	2.00	0.67	2500	544-8888
Prudential Equity-Income B		14,290			20	-6	26	8	20	— [1][2]	2.02	1000	225-1852
SAFECO Income		13,833			19	-11	23	11	13	—	0.90	1000	426-6730
National Total Return		14,033			27	-6	29	10	NA	5.75 [1]	1.35	250	356-5535
Merrill Lynch Strategic Dividend B		12,963			23	-8	15	8	8	— [1][2]	1.91	1000	637-3863
United Income		14,255			27	-5	30	12	16	8.50	0.65	500	366-5465
Oppenheimer Equity-Income A		12,614			19	-1	17	7	15	5.75 [1]	0.82	1000	525-7048
Delaware Decatur II		13,175			27	-8	20	8	15	5.75 [1]	1.21	250	523-4640
Putnam Equity Income A		12,595			16	-7	25	5	17	5.75 [1]	1.20	500	225-1581
Delaware Decatur I		12,219			21	-12	22	9	15	8.50	0.71	250	523-4640

GROWTH-AND-INCOME

Fund name	Score	5 years	Risk '87	Risk '90	Yearly performance '89	'90	'91	'92	'93	Load	Expense	Minimum	Phone 800-
Vista Growth & Income A		$22,331	—	◗	57%	0%	59%	15%	13%	4.75% [1]	1.39%	$2500	348-4782
AIM Value A		17,900	○	●	32	2	43	16	19	5.50 [1]	1.19	500	347-1919
Neuberger & Berman Guardian		17,063	○	○	22	−5	34	19	14	—	0.84	1000	877-9700
Fidelity Growth & Income		16,529	○	○	30	−7	42	12	20	2.00	0.86	2500	544-8888
Clipper		15,851	●	○	22	−8	33	16	11	—	1.17	5000	776-5033
IDS Managed Retirement		16,515	○	○	35	0	46	9	15	5.00	0.85	2000	328-8300
Selected American		16,113	○	●	20	−4	46	6	6	— [1]	1.19	1000	243-1575
Scudder Growth & Income		15,094	○	●	26	−2	28	10	16	—	0.95	1000	225-2470
Franklin Rising Dividends		15,448	◗	◗	20	0	36	10	−4	4.00 [1]	1.38	100	342-5236
Mutual Qualified [4]		15,135	○	○	14	−10	21	23	23	—	0.84	1000	553-3014
AIM Charter		15,421	○	◗	38	8	38	1	9	5.50 [1]	1.17	500	347-1919
Gateway Index Plus		14,486	◗	◗	19	10	18	5	7	—	1.13	1000	354-6339
▲ S&P 500		15,440	○	○	32	−3	31	8	10	—	—	—	—
Vanguard Quantitative		15,434	○	○	32	−2	30	7	14	—	0.43	3000	662-7447
AARP Growth & Income		14,886	○	◗	27	−2	26	9	16	—	0.91	500	253-2277
Rightime		13,597	●	◗	11	1	30	4	8	— [1]	2.60	2000	242-1421
Vanguard Index 500		15,333	○	○	31	−3	30	7	10	—	0.20	3000	662-7447
IDS Strategy Equity		15,278	○	○	21	−6	28	13	16	— [1][2]	1.63	2000	328-8300
Vanguard/Windsor II		15,171	○	◗	28	−10	29	12	14	—	0.41	3000	662-7447
John Hancock Sovereign Inv. A		14,724	○	○	24	4	30	7	6	5.00 [1]	1.15	1000	225-5291
Dean Witter Value-Added Market		14,934	—	●	23	−12	32	13	13	— [1][2]	1.80	1000	869-3863
T. Rowe Price Growth & Income		15,275	○	○	19	−11	32	15	13	—	0.90	2500	638-5660
PaineWebber Dividend Growth A		14,659	○	○	25	0	35	4	−3	4.50 [1]	1.22	1000	647-1568
Founders Blue Chip		14,450	○	◗	36	0	28	0	14	— [1]	1.24	1000	525-2440

1. 12b-1 fee. 2. Deferred sales charge. 3. 415-434-0311. 4. Closed to new investors at time of study. 5. 414-272-6133. 6. 212-245-4500. 7. Redemption fee if you sell within one year. 8. 314-727-5305. 9. Redemption fee when you sell.

Data source: Morningstar, Inc.

GROWTH-AND-INCOME Continued

Fund name	Score	5 years	Risk '87	Risk '90	'89	'90	'91	'92	'93	Load	Expense	Minimum	Phone 800-
Dreyfus	▮	14,165	◐	○	24	-3	28	6	6	—	0.78	2500	645-6561
Stagecoach Corporate Stock	▮	14,803	○	○	30	-4	29	6	9	—[1]	0.97	1000	222-8222
Oppenheimer Total Return A	▮	14,899	○	◐	19	-4	36	13	21	5.75 [1]	0.93	1000	525-7048
Evergreen Total Return	▮	14,033	◐	○	17	-6	23	12	13	—	1.19	2000	235-0064
Dean Witter Dividend Growth	▮	14,833	—	◐	31	-7	31	6	14	—[1][2]	1.40	1000	869-3863
Kemper Blue Chip	▮	14,085	—		27	2	44	-1	3	5.75	1.66	1000	621-1048
Fidelity	▮	14,587	○	○	29	-5	24	8	18	—	0.68	2500	544-8888
IDS Stock	▮	14,444	○	○	30	2	28	7	17	5.00	0.72	2000	328-8300
FPA Paramount [4]	▮	14,201	○	◐	23	2	24	10	21	6.50	0.92	1500	982-4372
IDS Equity Plus	▮	14,804	◐	○	29	-3	32	10	15	5.00	0.74	2000	328-8300
MFS Lifetime Total Return	▮	13,977	◐	●	16	2	20	7	NA	—[1][2]	2.22	1000	225-2606
Dodge & Cox Stock	▮	14,398	○	○	27	-5	21	11	18	—	0.64	2500	[3]
Massachusetts Investors A	▮	14,570	○	○	36	0	28	7	10	5.75[1]	0.61	1000	225-2606
Salomon Brothers Investors	▮	14,381	○	○	22	-6	29	7	15	—	0.70	500	725-6666
Investment Company of America	▮	14,231	○	○	29	1	27	7	12	5.75[1]	0.59	250	421-0180
State Street Investment C	▮	$14,360	○	○	32%	-1%	28%	6%	10%	4.50%	0.50%	$ 250	882-0052
Rightime Blue Chip	▮	12,890	●	◐	20	1	23	4	7	4.75[1]	2.17	2000	242-1421
American Leaders A	▮	14,182	○	●	12	-2	31	12	12	4.50	1.06	500	245-5051
Seligman Common Stock A	▮	14,516	○	◐	27	-4	30	11	15	4.75[1]	0.72	1000	221-2783
United Retirement	▮	14,013	○	○	23	2	22	13	13	8.50	0.82	500	366-5465
Putnam Fund for Gro. & Income A	▮	14,039	○	○	21	2	19	12	14	5.75[1]	1.07	500	225-1581
Colonial A	▮	13,916	○	○	20	-8	26	13	14	5.75[1]	1.05	1000	248-2828
Cardinal	▮	14,136	○	○	22	-6	32	10	6	6.00	0.67	1000	848-7734
Penn Square Mutual	▮	14,002	◐	○	26	-5	28	9	13	4.75[1]	0.95	500	523-8440
Merrill Lynch Capital A	▮	13,505	○	○	23	1	25	5	14	6.50	0.54	250	637-3863

Fund name	Score (0–100)	Risk '87	Risk '90	5 years	'89	'90	'91	'92	'93	Load	Expense	Minimum	Phone 800-
American Mutual		◐	○	13,430	25	-2	22	8	14	5.75 [1]	0.63	250	421-0180
Strong Total Return		●	◐	12,714	3	-7	34	1	23	—	1.30	250	368-1030
American Capital Comstock A		◐	○	14,398	31	-3	32	7	9	5.75 [1]	0.82	500	421-5666
Fundamental Investors		○	○	14,371	29	-6	30	10	18	5.75 [1]	0.69	250	421-0180
Washington Mutual Investors		○	○	13,902	29	-4	24	9	13	5.75 [1]	0.74	250	421-0180
Putnam Managed Income		○	○	13,762	18	-3	24	11	12	5.75 [1]	1.11	500	225-1581
Nationwide		○	◐	14,088	34	0	30	3	7	7.50	0.60	250	848-0920
Alliance Growth & Income A		○	◐	13,669	26	-2	27	5	10	5.50 [1]	1.14	250	227-4618
Keystone Custodian S-1		○	○	13,583	29	-5	29	0	10	— [1][2]	2.08	1000	343-2898
Affiliated		○	○	13,602	24	-5	22	13	13	5.75 [1]	0.58	250	874-3733
Sentinel Common Stock		○	○	13,635	28	-3	31	6	9	8.50	0.71	500	282-3863
Common Sense Gro. & Income		○	○	13,721	27	-3	31	7	9	8.50	1.14	250	544-5445
American Capital Growth & Inc. A		◐	○	13,673	16	-5	30	10	16	5.75 [1]	1.14	500	421-5666
Smith Barney Income & Growth A		○	●	13,297	25	-10	26	7	16	4.50 [1]	0.97	3000	544-7835
Pioneer		○	○	13,481	23	-11	23	14	14	5.75 [1]	0.87	50	225-6292
Merrill Lynch Basic Value A		○	●	12,948	18	-13	27	10	22	6.50	0.58	250	637-3863
Pioneer II		○	●	13,117	22	-12	26	9	19	5.75 [1]	0.85	50	225-6292

GROWTH

Fund name	Score (0–100)	Risk '87	Risk '90	5 years	'89	'90	'91	'92	'93	Load	Expense	Minimum	Phone 800-
CGM Capital Development [4]		○	●	$22,934	18%	1%	99%	17%	29%	—	0.86%	$1000	345-4048
Berger 100		◐◐	○	21,714	48	-6	89	9	21	— [1]	1.89	250	333-1001
Fidelity Contrafund		○	○	20,810	43	4	55	16	21	3.00%	0.86	2500	544-8888
Janus Twenty [4]		◐	○	20,432	51	1	69	2	3	—	1.01	1000	525-8983
MainStay Capital Appreciation		○	○	19,785	26	4	68	11	14	— [1][2]	2.00	500	522-4202
Fidelity Blue Chip Growth		—	○	17,807	36	4	55	6	25	3.00	1.27	2500	544-8888
Janus		○	○	17,819	46	-1	43	7	11	—	0.96	1000	525-8983

1 12b-1 fee.   2 Deferred sales charge.   3 415-434-0311.   4 Closed to new investors at time of study.   5 414-272-6133.   6 212-245-4500.   7 Redemption fee if you sell within one year.   8 314-727-5305.   9 Redemption fee when you sell.

Data source: Morningstar, Inc.

GROWTH Continued

Fund name	Score	Risk '87	Risk '90	5 years	'89	'90	'91	'92	'93	Load	Expense	Minimum	Phone 800-
Monetta		O	◑	18,476	15	11	56	5	0	—	1.41	100	666-3882
Twentieth Century Growth		O	●	17,287	43	-4	69	-4	4	—	1.00	0	345-2021
Westcore MIDCO Growth Instl.		O	●	18,482	29	4	67	6	17	4.50	0.83	1000	392-2673
Fidelity Advisor Gro. Opp.		—	●	17,298	24	-2	43	15	22	4.75 [1]	1.60	2500	522-7297
T. Rowe Price New America Gro.		O	●	18,326	38	-12	62	10	17	—	1.25	2500	638-5660
Fidelity Growth Company		O	●	18,266	42	4	48	8	16	3.00	1.09	2500	544-8888
Gabelli Growth		◑	◑	16,866	40	-2	34	4	11	— [1]	1.35	1000	422-3554
Pasadena Growth A		O	●	18,514	38	-5	68	3	-6	5.50	1.80	2500	882-2855
Value Line		O	◑	17,230	31	-1	53	5	7	—	0.71	1000	223-0818
Vanguard U.S. Growth		O	●	17,295	38	5	47	3	-1	—	0.49	3000	662-7447
IDEX II Growth A		O	●	17,578	45	-1	59	1	4	5.50 [1]	1.63	50	624-4339
SteinRoe Stock		O	O	17,188	35	1	46	8	3	—	0.92	1000	338-2550
Dean Witter American Value		O	O	17,039	25	-1	56	4	19	— [1][2]	1.77	1000	869-3863
IDS New Dimensions		O	O	16,897	32	5	51	5	14	5.00	0.95	2000	328-8300
Nicholas		O	O	16,760	25	-5	42	13	6	—	0.76	500	[5]
Sequoia [4]		◉	O	16,148	28	-4	40	9	11	—	1.00	1000	[6]
SteinRoe Special		O	O	16,960	38	-6	34	14	20	—	0.99	1000	338-2550
Kemper Growth		O	O	17,041	31	-4	67	-2	2	5.75	1.03	1000	621-1048
New York Venture		O	O	$16,749	35%	-3%	41%	12%	16%	4.75% [1]	0.91%	$1000	279-0279
Neuberger & Berman Sel. Sect.		O	O	16,262	30	-6	25	21	16	—	0.91	1000	877-9700
Thomson Growth B		O	O	16,204	37	0	42	2	9	— [1][7]	1.90	1000	227-7337
Columbia Growth		◑	O	16,040	29	-3	34	12	13	—	0.86	1000	547-1707
Piper Jaffray Value		O	O	16,578	39	1	48	3	5	4.00 [1]	1.29	250	866-7778
Neuberger & Berman Manhattan		O	O	16,263	29	-8	31	18	10	—	1.10	1000	877-9700
IDEX		O	●	16,897	43	-1	62	0	4	8.50	1.24	50	624-4339

Fund	Rating	Value						Sales charge	Expense	Min.	Phone
G.T. America Growth A	●	17,335	55	-7	19	32	8	4.75 [1]	2.00	500	824-1580
IDEX 3 [4]	○	16,719	43	-2	62	0	5	8.50	1.21	50	624-4339
IDS Growth	◐	17,004	37	3	47	8	9	5.00	0.88	2000	328-8300
Kemper Investment Growth	○	16,261	31	-2	57	-3	5	— [1][2]	2.07	250	621-1048
IAI Regional	○	15,694	31	0	35	4	9	— [1]	1.25	5000	945-3863
Fortis Growth	◐	17,119	43	-6	68	1	10	4.75 [1]	1.13	500	800-2638
Fidelity Retirement Growth	●	16,457	30	-10	46	11	22	—	1.06	500	544-8888
Fidelity Trend	○	16,504	32	-13	36	17	19	—	0.50	2500	544-8888
Gabelli Asset	◐	15,088	27	-6	18	15	22	— [1]	1.28	1000	422-3554
Mutual Beacon	●	15,139	17	-8	18	23	23	—	0.85	5000	553-3014
Oppenheimer Special A	○	16,149	21	-3	44	13	3	5.75 [1]	0.90	1000	525-7048
Dreyfus Appreciation	○	15,617	27	-2	38	4	1	— [1]	1.30	2500	242-8671
Dreyfus Third Century	○	15,395	17	3	38	2	5	—	1.08	2500	645-6561
Fidelity Magellan	◐	16,182	35	-5	41	7	25	3.00	0.99	2500	544-8888
Neuberger & Berman Partners	○	15,175	23	-5	22	18	16	—	0.86	1000	877-9700
Strong Opportunity	○	15,212	18	-11	32	17	21	—	1.60	1000	368-1030
Gintel	○	15,705	24	-7	16	25	2	—	1.40	5000	243-5808
Mutual Shares [4]	◐	15,028	15	-10	21	21	21	—	0.82	5000	553-3014
▲ S&P 500		15,440	32	-3	31	8	10	—	—	—	—
Fidelity Value	○	15,653	23	-13	26	21	23	—	1.00	2500	544-8888
MFS Managed Sectors B	◐	16,476	40	-14	60	4	4	— [1][2]	2.34	1000	225-2606
T. Rowe Price Cap. App.	●	14,527	21	-1	22	9	16	—	1.11	2500	638-5660
Invesco Growth	○	15,680	31	-1	42	3	18	— [1]	1.04	250	525-8085
WPG Tudor	◐	15,901	25	-5	46	5	13	—	1.21	2500	223-3332
AIM Weingarten	◐	15,797	36	6	47	-1	2	5.50 [1]	1.10	500	347-1919

1. 12b-1 fee. 2. Deferred sales charge. 3. 415-434-0311. 4. Closed to new investors at time of study. 5. 414-272-6133. 6. 212-245-4500. 7. Redemption fee if you sell within one year. 8. 314-727-5305. 9. Redemption fee when you sell.

Data source: Morningstar, Inc.

GROWTH Continued

Fund name	Score	5 years	Risk '87	Risk '90	'89	'90	'91	'92	'93	Load	Expense	Minimum	Phone 800-
Twentieth Century Heritage		15,873	—	O	35	−9	36	10	20	—	1.00	0	345-2021
Vanguard/Morgan Growth		15,426	O	O	23	−2	29	10	7	—	0.49	3000	662-7447
Putnam Vista A		15,756	O	●	26	−7	37	18	17	5.75 ①	0.96	500	225-1581
Composite Northwest 50		16,307	O	●	38	−1	44	4	2	4.50 ①	1.12	1000	543-8072
Fortis Capital		15,606	O	●	38	−9	49	7	3	4.75 ①	1.23	500	800-2638
Fidelity Destiny II		16,268	O	◐	26	−3	41	15	27	8.24	0.88	50	752-2347
Keystone Custodian K-2		15,530	O	●	24	−7	42	8	13	— ①②	1.62	1000	343-2898
Guardian Park Avenue		15,593	O	●	24	−12	35	20	20	4.50	0.68	1000	221-3253
MFS Capital Growth B		15,432	O	◐	29	−2	30	8	4	— ①②	2.26	1000	225-2606
Seligman Growth A		15,557	O	●	34	−5	38	11	6	4.75 ①	0.76	1000	221-2783
Scudder Capital Growth		15,559	O	●	34	−17	43	7	20	—	1.04	1000	225-2470
Fidelity Advisor Strat. Opp.		14,492	O	◐	33	−7	23	13	20	4.75 ①	1.46	2500	522-7297
Lindner		14,099	●	O	21	−11	23	13	20	— ⑦	0.80	2000	Ⓑ
Quest For Value A		15,145	O	●	20	−7	33	18	7	5.50 ①	1.72	1000	232-3863
Security Equity		15,281	O	●	32	−6	35	11	15	5.75	1.06	100	888-2461
Phoenix Growth		14,342	O	◐	27	6	28	4	4	4.75 ①	1.20	500	243-4361
Merrill Lynch Growth for Inv. B		$15,123	O	●	32%	−1%	24%	9%	31%	— ①②	1.88%	$1000	637-3863
Smith Barney Shearson Sec. An. B		13,628	●	●	22	−7	31	8	5	— ①②	2.10	1000	451-2010
Fidelity Destiny I		15,738	◐	●	26	−3	39	15	26	8.24%	0.61	50	752-2347
Mathers		12,692	●	O	10	10	9	3	2	—	0.94	1000	962-3863
T. Rowe Price Growth Stock		14,687	O	◐	25	−4	34	6	16	—	0.86	2500	638-5660
Dreyfus Strategic Investing A		13,586	◐	◐	32	1	41	−5	17	4.50 ①	1.93	2500	645-6561

Fund	Value	Rating						Load	Expense	Min.	Phone
Mass. Investors Growth Stock A	15,556	○	38	−6	48	6	14	5.75⊡	0.64	1000	225-2606
American Capital Enterprise A	15,336	◑	31	−3	39	8	11	5.75⊡	0.97	500	421-5666
Keystone Custodian S-3	15,093	○	25	−9	43	5	9	—⊡②	1.69	1000	343-2898
Dreyfus Growth Opportunity	14,312	○	15	−7	51	−4	2	—	0.95	2500	645-6561
AIM Summit	15,333	◐	31	1	44	5	8	8.50	0.74	50	347-1919
Prudential Equity B	14,973	◑	32	−4	24	13	21	—⊡②	1.71	1000	225-1852
AARP Capital Growth	15,041	○	33	−16	41	5	16	—	1.13	500	253-2277
Alliance A	15,286	◑	23	−4	34	15	14	5.50⊡	0.83	250	227-4618
Merrill Lynch Fund for Tom. B	14,620	○	29	−8	31	5	10	—⊡②	1.93	500	637-3863
Twentieth Century Select	14,115	○	40	0	32	−4	15	—	1.00	0	345-2021
New Economy	14,874	◐	32	−10	29	17	31	5.75⊡	0.92	1000	421-0180
Growth Fund of America	14,898	○	30	−4	36	7	15	5.75⊡	0.79	1000	421-0180
Smith Barney Shearson App. A	14,199	○	30	0	27	6	8	5.00⊡	0.80	1000	451-2010
First Union Value B Inv.	14,166	○	27	−3	25	8	9	4.00⊡	0.98	1000	326-3241
Delaware DelCap	14,981	○	34	−4	42	2	12	5.75⊡	1.43	250	523-4640
Franklin Growth	13,659	◑	24	2	27	3	8	4.00	0.66	100	342-5236
TNE Growth A 4	14,444	○	22	5	57	−7	11	6.50⊡	1.14	2500	343-7104
Legg Mason Value	14,492	○	20	−17	35	11	11	—⊡	1.90	1000	822-5544
Phoenix Equity Opp.	14,525	○	27	−7	23	17	13	5.75⊡	1.36	250	243-4361
MFS Research A	14,399	○	26	−6	33	11	22	5.75⊡	0.85	1000	225-2606
Gradison-McDonald Est. Value	13,554	◐	16	−8	22	10	21	—⊡	1.31	1000	869-5999
Colonial Growth Shares A	14,721	○	29	−11	34	11	10	5.75⊡	1.15	1000	248-2828
AMCAP	14,494	○	27	−4	37	7	11	5.75⊡	0.75	1000	421-0180
Lord Abbett Value Appreciation	14,187	○	20	−5	27	13	14	5.75⊡	1.14	1000	874-3733
Oppenheimer	14,380	◑	24	−4	29	14	15	5.75⊡	1.09	1000	525-7048
Babson Growth	13,994	○	22	−9	26	9	10	—	0.86	500	422-2766

1 12b-1 fee. 2 Deferred sales charge. 3 415-434-0311. 4 Closed to new investors at time of study. 5 414-272-6133. 6 212-245-4500. 7 Redemption fee if you sell within one year. 8 314-727-5305. 9 Redemption fee when you sell.

Data source: Morningstar, Inc.

GROWTH Continued

Fund name	Score	5 years	Risk '87	Risk '90	'89	'90	'91	'92	'93	Load	Expense	Minimum	Phone 800-
Oppenheimer Time		13,843	○	○	28	-7	39	2	20	5.75 ⊥	0.96	1000	525-7048
Harbor Growth		14,254	●	●	23	-7	50	-6	18	—	0.89	2000	422-1050
Ivy Growth A		13,817	○	◑	27	-4	31	5	12	5.75 ⊥	1.31	1000	456-5111
Putnam Investors A		14,254	○	○	34	-3	29	8	18	5.75 ⊥	0.94	500	225-1581
Pilgrim MagnaCap		13,685	○	⊕	22	-3	25	8	11	1.00 ⊥	1.60	1000	334-3444
Common Sense Growth		14,418	○	●	28	-3	39	7	9	8.50	1.26	250	544-5445
Smith Barney Shearson Dir. Val. B		13,784	○	◑	23	-7	22	9	9	— ①②	1.80	1000	451-2010
Princor Capital Accumulation		13,694	○	●	15	-11	37	9	8	5.00 ⊥	0.92	300	451-5447
United Accumulative		13,429	○	○	28	-10	24	14	9	8.50	0.63	500	366-5465
American Capital Pace A		13,626	○	●	29	-6	31	4	11	5.75 ⊥	1.00	500	421-5666
Nationwide Growth		13,440	○	●	15	-8	36	6	11	7.50	0.65	250	848-0920
AIM Growth A		13,626	○	●	29	-5	37	0	4	5.50 ⊥	1.19	500	347-1919
Boston Company Cap. App. Retail		12,899	○	○	24	-13	23	4	17	— ⊥	1.22	1000	225-5267
MFS Growth Opportunities A		13,274	◑	●	28	-4	22	8	16	5.75 ⊥	0.88	1000	225-2606
IDS Progressive		13,240	○	●	11	-18	25	20	12	5.00	1.06	2000	328-8300
Prudential Growth B		12,867	○	●	22	-10	24	3	8	— ①②	2.15	1000	225-1852
Franklin Equity		12,873	○	◑	17	-9	27	4	9	4.00	0.70	100	342-5236
United Vanguard		12,513	○	●	19	-4	27	3	14	8.50	0.96	500	366-5465
Security Action		12,784	○	◑	19	-10	34	5	NA	8.50	0.78	50	888-2461

AGGRESSIVE-GROWTH

Fund name	Score	5 years	Risk '87	Risk '90	'89	'90	'91	'92	'93	Load	Expense	Minimum	Phone 800-
Kaufmann		$24,161	◐	●	47%	-6%	79%	11%	18%	— [1][9]	3.04%	$1500	237-0132
Thomson Opportunity B [4]		22,067	○	◐	31	-7	68	28	36	— [1][7]	2.00	1000	227-7337
Strong Discovery		18,125	—	○	24	-3	69	2	22	—	1.40	1000	368-1030
AIM Constellation		20,043	●	●	38	-4	70	15	17	5.50% [1]	1.20	500	347-1919
Founders Special		18,311	○	○	39	-10	64	8	16	—	1.27	1000	525-2440
Invesco Dynamics		18,666	◐	●	23	-6	67	13	19	— [1]	1.18	250	525-8085
Keystone Custodian S-4		18,913	●	●	24	-6	73	10	25	— [1][2]	1.47	1000	343-2898
Delaware Trend		19,673	●	●	50	-25	74	22	22	5.75 [1]	1.18	250	523-4640
Pacific Horizon Agg. Growth		17,666	○	●	37	5	71	-2	7	4.50 [1]	1.44	1000	332-3863
MetLife-State St. Cap. Apprec. A		17,994	○	○	32	-14	74	9	23	4.50 [1]	1.50	250	882-0052
Seligman Capital A		17,682	◐	●	32	1	55	12	5	4.75 [1]	1.01	1000	221-2783
Putnam Voyager A		16,841	○	●	35	-3	50	10	18	5.75 [1]	1.20	500	225-1581
▲ S&P 500		15,440	○	○	32	-3	31	8	10	—	—	—	—
IDS Strategy Aggressive Equity		16,159	◐	●	33	-1	51	-1	8	— [1][2]	1.75	2000	328-8300
Value Line Leveraged Growth		15,282	○	○	32	-2	46	-2	16	—	0.96	1000	223-0818
Oppenheimer Target		15,795	●	●	18	-2	41	10	4	5.75 [1]	1.05	1000	525-7048
Dreyfus Capital Growth (Prem.)		14,040	○	○	20	-1	33	6	15	3.00	1.07	2500	645-6561
Smith Barney Shearson Ag. Gr. A		14,973	●	●	41	-6	42	2	21	5.00 [1]	1.05	1000	451-2010
USAA Mutual Aggressive Growth		14,650	○	●	17	-12	72	-9	8	—	0.82	1000	382-8722
Fidelity Capital Appreciation		13,148	○	◐	27	-16	10	16	33	3.00	0.71	2500	544-8888
Alliance Quasar A		12,433	●	●	28	-23	34	3	16	5.50 [1]	1.62	250	227-4170

1 12b-1 fee. 2 Deferred sales charge. 3 415-434-0311. 4 Closed to new investors at time of study. 5 414-272-6133. 6 212-245-4500. 7 Redemption fee if you sell within one year. 8 314-727-5305. 9 Redemption fee when you sell.

Data source: Morningstar, Inc.

SMALL-COMPANY

Fund name	Score	5 years	Risk '87	Risk '90	'89	'90	'91	'92	'93	Load	Expense	Minimum	Phone 800-
Twentieth Century Ultra Investors		$21,995	○	◐	37%	9%	86%	1%	22%	—	1.00%	$ 0	345-2021
Skyline Special Equities [4]		21,487	○	●	24	-9	47	41	23	—	1.53	1000	458-5222
Alger Small Capitalization		20,966	●	●	65	7	55	4	13	—[1][2]	2.20	0	992-3863
Robertson Stephens Emer. Gro.		18,911	—	◐	44	10	59	-3	7	—[1]	1.37	5000	766-3863
MFS Emerging Growth B		21,349	○	●	27	-3	88	12	24	—[1][2]	2.28	1000	225-2606
Janus Venture [4]		18,129	◐	●	39	0	48	7	9	—	1.00	1000	525-8983
Nicholas Limited Edition [4]		17,847	◐	●	17	-2	44	17	9	—	0.86	2000	[5]
Oppenheimer Discovery		18,681	○	●	34	-15	72	17	18	5.75% [1]	1.34	1000	525-7048
Legg Mason Special Investment		18,146	○	●	32	1	39	15	24	—[1]	2.10	1000	822-5544
Fidelity OTC		17,929	○	◐	30	-5	49	15	8	3.00	1.17	2500	544-8888
Acorn [4]		17,643	○	●	25	-18	47	24	32	[7]	0.71	4000	922-6769
Keystone Amer. Hartwell Emer. Gr. A		18,878	●	●	39	3	73	1	4	4.75% [1]	1.56	1000	343-2898
Sit Growth		17,367	○	◐	35	-2	65	-2	9	—	0.83	2000	332-5580
Scudder Development		17,644	○	●	23	1	72	-2	9	—	1.30	1000	225-2470
American Cap. Emerging Gro. A		17,666	○	●	29	2	60	10	24	5.75 [1]	1.14	500	421-5666
Babson Enterprise [4]		17,591	◐	●	22	-16	43	25	16	—	1.17	1000	422-2766
Columbia Special		18,275	◐	●	32	-12	50	14	22	—	1.19	2000	547-1707
IDS Discovery		17,182	◐	●	31	0	53	9	10	5.00	1.04	2000	328-8300
United New Concepts		17,311	○	●	9	2	88	5	11	8.50	1.23	500	366-5465
Vanguard Explorer		16,693	—	●	9	-11	56	13	15	—	0.69	3000	662-7447
Vanguard Index Extended Market [4]		15,663	—	◐	24	-14	42	12	14	—	0.21	3000	662-7447
T. Rowe Price New Horizons		16,842	◐	●	26	-10	52	11	22	—	0.96	2500	638-5660
Dreyfus New Leaders		16,396	◐	●	31	-12	45	9	17	—[7]	1.29	2500	645-6561

Fund name	Score	5 years	Risk '87	Risk '90	'89	'90	'91	'92	'93	Load	Expense	Minimum $	Phone 800-
Twentieth Century Vista Inv.		$17,049	●	○	52%	-16%	74%	-2%	5%	—	1.00%	0	345-2021
▲ S&P 500		15,440	○	○	32	-3	31	8	10	—	—	—	—
Prudential Growth Opportunity B		16,502	●	◐	19	-12	39	20	19	— [1][2]	2.16	1000	225-1852
Nicholas II		15,435	◐	○	18	-6	40	9	6	—	0.66	1000	[5]
Pennsylvania Mutual		15,200	◐	◐	17	-12	32	16	11	— [7]	0.91	2000	221-4268
Kemper Small Cap. Equity		16,040	●	●	26	-5	69	0	17	5.75	1.27	1000	621-1048
MFS Emerging Growth		16,783	●	●	26	-11	70	8	NA	5.75 [1]	1.43	1000	225-2606
Pioneer Three		15,488	●	◐	20	-13	36	20	16	5.75 [1]	0.74	1000	225-6292
Vanguard Small Cap. Stock		15,591	●	◐	11	-18	45	18	19	—	0.18	3000	662-7447
Evergreen		14,704	●	○	15	-12	40	8	6	—	1.13	2000	235-0064
T. Rowe Price Over-the-Counter		14,742	●	○	19	-20	39	14	18	—	1.34	2500	638-5660
SAFECO Growth		14,870	●	○	19	-15	63	-3	22	—	0.91	1000	426-6730
Royce Value		14,348	●	○	16	-14	31	16	11	2.50 [1][2]	1.81	2000	221-4268
Putnam OTC Emerging Growth A		15,336	●	◐	29	-10	41	13	32	5.75 [1]	1.39	500	225-1581
Calvert-Ariel Growth [4]		14,455	●	○	25	-16	33	12	9	4.75 [1]	1.23	2000	368-2748

INTERNATIONAL AND GLOBAL

Fund name	Score	5 years	Risk '87	Risk '90	Yearly performance '89	'90	'91	'92	'93	Load	Expense	Minimum	Phone 800-
Scudder Global		$13,723	—	○	37%	-6%	17%	4%	31%	—	1.59%	$1000	225-2470
Harbor International		13,726	—	○	37	-10	21	0	45	—	1.23	2000	422-1050
EuroPacific Growth		12,767	—	○	24	0	19	2	36	5.75 [1]	1.24	250	421-0180
New Perspective		12,952	●	●	26	-2	23	4	27	5.75 [1]	0.86	250	421-0180
Scudder International		11,618	—	◐	27	-9	12	-3	37	—	1.30	1000	225-2470

1 12b-1 fee.   2 Deferred sales charge.   3 415-434-0311.   4 Closed to new investors at time of study.   5 414-272-6133.   6 212-245-4500.   7 Redemption fee if you sell within one year.   8 314-727-5305.   9 Redemption fee when you sell.

Data source: Morningstar, Inc.

INTERNATIONAL AND GLOBAL Continued

Fund name	Score	Risk '87	Risk '90	5 years	'89	'90	'91	'92	'93	Load	Expense	Minimum	Phone 800-
T. Rowe Price International Stock		—	○	11,700	24	-9	16	-3	40	—	1.10	2500	638-5660
Templeton Foreign		—	●	12,502	31	-3	18	0	37	5.75	0.94	500	237-0738
Templeton Growth		—	●	13,320	23	-9	31	4	33	5.75	0.88	500	237-0738
Merrill Lynch Pacific A		—	◐	10,473	15	-10	18	-8	34	6.50	1.01	250	637-3863
Oppenheimer Global A		—	●	11,885	35	-1	27	-14	43	5.75[1]	1.35	1000	525-7048
Merrill Lynch Global A		—	●	11,688	24	-9	17	4	24	6.50	1.49	1000	637-3863
Merrill Lynch EuroFund B		—	◑	11,419	25	-3	15	-6	31	—[1][2]	2.16	500	637-3863
G.T. Pacific Growth A		—	◐	11,337	48	-11	13	-8	61	4.75[1]	2.00	500	824-1580
Templeton Smaller Co. Growth		—	○	13,183	18	-16	40	4	32	5.75	1.33	500	237-0738
International Equity		—	○	10,499	22	-11	4	-3	46	—	0.75	2500	344-8332
Fidelity Europe		—	○	10,859	32	-5	4	-3	27	3.00	1.22	2500	544-8888
Dean Witter World Wide Invest.		—	◑	10,982	17	-10	19	-7	41	—[1][2]	2.39	1000	869-3863
Vanguard Int. Growth		—	◑	10,176	25	-12	5	-6	45	—	0.58	3000	662-7447
Templeton World		—	●	12,317	23	-16	30	3	34	5.75	0.86	500	237-0738
Putnam Global Growth A		—	●	11,412	25	-9	18	0	32	5.75[1]	1.47	500	225-1581
First Investors Global		—	●	11,077	38	-12	17	-5	23	6.90[1]	1.84	2000	423-4026
G.T. International Growth A		—	●	10,856	39	-14	13	-6	34	4.75[1]	1.90	500	824-1580
IDS International		—	◑	10,383	18	-6	12	-6	32	5.00	1.45	2000	328-8300
Kemper International		—	●	10,232	19	-7	9	-5	36	5.75	1.41	1000	621-1048
Fidelity Overseas		—	○	9,569	17	-7	9	-11	40	3.00	1.52	2500	544-8888
Prudential Global B		—	●	9,939	12	-17	12	-5	48	—[1][2]	2.32	1000	225-1852
United International Growth		—	●	10,252	13	-14	19	-1	46	8.50	1.18	500	366-5465
Alliance International A		—	●	9,781	30	-21	8	-6	28	5.50[1]	1.82	250	227-4618
G.T. Europe Growth A		—	●	9,426	41	-15	4	-11	28	4.75[1]	2.10	500	824-1580

[1] 12b-1 fee. [2] Deferred sales charge. [3] 415-434-0311. [4] Closed to new investors at time of study. [5] 414-272-6133. [6] 212-245-4500. [7] Redemption fee if you sell within one year. [8] 314-727-5305. [9] Redemption fee when you sell.

Data source: Morningstar, Inc.

RATINGS OF BOND MUTUAL FUNDS

Listed by type: corporate, government, and municipal. Corporate bond funds are further divided by maturity. Corporate high-yield funds are also listed separately, as are government funds that invest in mortgages. Within each group, listed by overall score.

The entry in each group designated by a ▶ shows how three-month Treasury bills, an essentially risk-free investment, would have scored for the five years under study. For municipal bond funds, we adjusted the return on three-month Treasury bills to account for municipal bonds' tax advantages (based on a 28 percent federal income-tax bracket).

Score. Based half on the fund's performance, as measured by its five-year accumulation, and half on its risk score.

5 years. How much an investor would have accumulated by investing $2,000 a year in the fund at the beginning of each year, 1988 through 1992. Sales charges are deducted from each yearly investment; redemption fees, at the end of the five-year period.

Risk. We compared each fund's monthly

total return for 1988 through 1992 to the rate during each of those 60 months on three-month Treasury bills. We counted the number of months each fund lagged the T-bill rate, and the severity of that underperformance, then compared the results to the average for all funds. Funds with scores plus or minus 20 percent of the average got a ○. Scores up to 40 percent better than average earned a ◑; funds that scored at least 41 percent better earned a ●; funds that did 21 to 40 percent worse got a ◐. And the worst performers (41 percent or more below average) got a ●. (In some instances, funds with identical risk symbols may appear to be out of order based on their five-year accumulations; that's because our calculations of overall score use the actual numbers behind each risk symbol, which provide a more precise differentiation.)

Quality. The letter grade from AAA (highest) to B- (lowest) that approximates the average quality of the bonds in a fund's portfolio, as of 1993 study. That rating system is

explained in Table 2.1 on page 29. (Note that while these designations reflect the Standard & Poor's bond-rating system, Standard & Poor's uses a different methodology to rate bond funds, and its ratings may not match ours.)

Performance. The column headed '93 gives total return for 1993. NA indicates fund merged into another fund in 1993. The column headed '88–'92 shows the average annual total return from 1988 through 1992.

Load. Sales charge, if any, as of 1993 study. 12-b1 fees, deferred sales charges, or redemption fees are footnoted.

Expense. The percentage of the fund's assets each year that go toward administrative expenses, as of 1993 study.

Minimum. The minimum investment required to open an account. Subsequent investments may be much smaller. IRA accounts often have lower minimums.

Phone. Number to call for an application, prospectus, or other information.

As published in *Consumer Reports*, June 1993, and updated in January 1994.

CORPORATE: Short-term

Fund name	Score	5 years	Risk	Quality	Performance '93	Performance '88-'92	Load	Expense	Minimum	Phone 800-
Vanguard F.I. Short-Term Corp.		$13,336	◐	AA	7%	9.6%	—	0.27%	$3000	662-7447
Scudder Short-Term Bond		13,366	◐	AA	8	9.8	—	0.78	1000	225-2470
Strong Short-Term Bond		13,044	●	A	9	9.1	—	0.60	1000	368-1030
Fidelity Short-Term Bond		13,076	◐	BBB	9	8.6	—	0.75	2500	544-8888
Neuberger & Berman Ltd. Mat.		12,913	◐	AAA	7	8.8	—	0.65	5000	877-9700
Fidelity Adv. Short Fixed-Inc.		12,858	◐	A	9	8.3	1.50%[1]	0.90	2500	522-7297
T. Rowe Price Short-Term		12,705	◐	AA	7	8.0	—	0.79	2500	638-5660
Connecticut Mutual Income		12,753	◐	A	8	8.2	2.00	0.63	1000	322-2642
Neuberger & Bmn. Ultra Short		12,191	●	AAA	3	7.3	—	0.65	2000	877-9700
IAI Reserve		12,143	●	AA	3	7.0	—[1]	0.85	5000	945-3863
▲ Three-month Treasury bills		11,834	●	—	3	6.2	—	—	—	—

CORPORATE: Intermediate

Fund name	Score	5 years	Risk	Quality	Performance '93	Performance '88-'92	Load	Expense	Minimum	Phone 800-
Norwest Income Inv. A		$13,448	◐	AA	9%	9.8%	3.25%	0.13%	$1000	[7]
Columbia Fixed-Inc. Securities		13,907	○	AA	10	11.0	—	0.66	1000	547-1707

Fund	Value		Rating			Sales charge	Expense	Min.	Telephone
Vanguard Bond Index	13,618	○	AAA	10	10.4	—	0.20	3000	662-7447
Bond Fund of America	13,492	○	A	14	10.1	4.75 [1]	0.73	1000	421-0180
UMB Bond	13,133	◑	NR	8	9.0	—	0.87	1000	422-2766
T. Rowe Price New Income	13,306	○	AA	69	9.8	—	0.87	2500	638-5660
Fidelity Intermediate Bond	13,208	◑	AA	12	9.4	—	0.58	2500	544-8888
Bartlett Fixed-Income	13,246	○	A	7	9.5	—	1.00	5000	800-4612
Merrill Lynch Interm. Term A	13,151	◑	A	12	9.5	2.00	0.62	1000	637-3863
Composite Income	12,888	◑	A	11	8.4	4.00 [1]	0.95	1000	543-8072
One Group Inc. Bond Fiduciary	13,225	○	AAA	8	8.9	— [1]	0.63	2500	338-4345
Twentieth Century L.T. Bond	13,473	○	AA	10	10.2	—	0.98	1000	345-2021
Pioneer Bond	12,918	◑	AA	11	9.0	4.50 [1]	1.09	1000	225-6292
MFS Bond A	13,016	○	BBB	14	9.5	4.75 [1]	0.87	1000	225-2606
Warburg, Pincus Fixed-Income	13,036	○	A	10	8.8	—	0.75	2500	888-6878
Sentinel Bond	$13,089	○	A	12%	9.5%	5.25%	0.78%	$500	282-3863
Merrill Lynch Corp. High-Q. A	13,010	○	AA	13	9.5	4.00	0.58	1000	637-3863
Three-month Treasury bills	11,835	●	—	3	6.2	—	—	—	—
Colonial Income A	12,831	○	A	12	8.9	4.75 [1]	1.24	1000	248-2828
Phoenix High-Quality Bond	12,847	○	AA	NA	8.7	4.75 [1]	0.78	500	243-4361
Transamerica Inv. Quality Bond A	12,887	○	AA	9	8.8	4.75 [1]	1.70	100	343-6840
Thomson Income B	12,445	○	BBB	7	7.4	— [1][2]	1.90	1000	227-7337
Strong Income	12,078	◐	A	17	5.9	—	1.30	1000	368-1030

Data source: Morningstar, Inc.

[1] 12b-1 fee. [2] Redemption fee if you sell within one year. [3] Deferred sales charge. [4] Closed to new investors at time of study. [5] Redemption fee when you sell. [6] Adjusted for 28% federal tax bracket. [7] 212-363-3300.

CORPORATE: Long-term

Fund name	Score (0–100)	5 years	Risk	Quality	Performance '93	Performance '88-'92	Load	Expense	Minimum	Phone 800-
Vanguard F.I. Long-Term Corp.		$14,479	◐	A	14%	12.2%	—	0.31%	$3000	662-7447
Invesco Select Income		13,828	◐	BBB	11	10.4	—[1]	1.14	1000	525-8085
Fidelity Investment Grade Bond		13,904	○	A	16	10.8	—	0.67	2500	544-8888
Scudder Income		13,744	○	AA	13	10.8	—	0.97	1000	225-2470
SteinRoe Income		13,603	○	BBB	13	10.2	—	0.83	1000	338-2550
Babson Bond L		13,591	○	AA	11	10.2	—	0.99	500	422-2766
Dreyfus A Bonds Plus		13,858	○	AA	15	10.9	—	0.88	2500	645-6561
Smith Barney Shearson Inv. Gr. B		14,168	◐	A	18	11.4	—[1][3]	1.58	1000	451-2010
SteinRoe Intermediate Bond		13,486	○	A	9	9.9	—	0.67	1000	338-2550
Dreyfus Strategic Income		13,676	○	A	15	10.9	3.00%[1]	0.85	2500	645-6561
PaineWebber Inv. Grade Inc. A		13,393	○	A	13	10.0	4.00[1]	1.01	1000	647-1568
IDS Bond		13,465	○	A	15	10.1	5.00	0.72	2000	328-8300
Putnam Income A		13,245	○	A	12	9.8	4.75[1]	0.97	500	225-1581
IDS Strategy Income		13,632	◐	A	16	9.9	—[1][3]	1.64	2000	328-8300
John Hancock Sovereign Bond A		13,083	◐●	A	11	9.6	4.50[1]	1.44	1000	225-5291
TNE Bond Income A		13,127	○	AA	12	9.4	4.50[1]	1.08	2500	343-7104
IDS Selective		13,151	○	AA	13	9.7	5.00	0.74	2000	328-8300
Janus Flexible Income		13,631	◐	BB	16	9.1	—	1.00	1000	525-8983
Kemper Income & Capital Pres.		12,984	○	A	12	9.2	4.50	0.82	1000	621-1048
American Capital Corp. Bond A		12,779	○	A	12	8.7	4.75[1]	1.00	500	421-5666

Fund name	5 years	Risk	Quality	'93	'88-'92	Load	Expense	Minimum	Phone 800-
▲ Three-month Treasury bills	11,834	●	—	3	6.2	—	—	—	—
Keystone Custodian B-2	13,001	○	BBB	14	8.3	—①	1.99	1000	343-2898
Keystone Custodian B-1	12,896	○	AA	9	8.7	—①③	2.01	1000	343-2898
AIM Income A	12,905	○	A	15	9.2	4.75①③	0.99	500	347-1919
United Bond	12,371	○	A	13	8.0	8.50	0.64	500	366-5465

CORPORATE: High-yield

Fund name	Score 0 25 50 75 100	5 years	Risk	Quality	Performance '93	'88-'92	Load	Expense	Minimum	Phone 800-
Merrill Lynch High-Income A		$15,496	○	B	17%	12.7%	4.00%	0.59%	$1000	637-3863
Fidelity Capital & Income		15,660	◑	NR	24	11.7	—②	0.83	2500	544-8888
Putnam High Yield A		14,601	◑	BB	19	10.5	4.75①	0.97	500	225-1581
Putnam High Yield Advantage		14,803	◑	B	21	10.7	4.75①	1.14	500	225-1581
Lord Abbett Bond-Debenture		14,439	◑	BBB	16	11.1	4.75①	0.84	1000	874-3733
MainStay Hi. Yield Corp. Bond		14,724	●	BB	22	10.3	—①③	1.90	500	522-4202
Oppenheimer High-Yield A		13,602	○	BB	21	9.4	4.75①	1.03	1000	525-7048
Vanguard F.I. High-Yield Corp.		14,047	◑	BB	18	9.9	—②	0.34	3000	662-7447
Delaware Delchester		14,283	●	B	17	9.9	4.75①	1.08	250	523-4640
Kemper High-Yield		14,435	●	B	20	10.1	4.50	0.82	1000	621-1048
Northeast Investors		13,791	◑	B-	24	9.0	—	1.44	1000	225-6704

1 12b-1 fee.   2 Redemption fee if you sell within one year.   3 Deferred sales charge.   4 Closed to new investors at time of study.   5 Redemption fee when you sell.   6 Adjusted for 28% federal tax bracket.

Data source: Morningstar, Inc.

CORPORATE: HIGH-YIELD Continued

Fund name	Score (0–100)	5 years	Risk	Quality	Performance '93	Performance '88–'92	Load	Expense	Minimum	Phone 800-
Prudential High-Yield B		$14,046	◐	B	17%	8.9%	—[1][3]	1.41%	$1000	225-1852
T. Rowe Price High-Yield		13,715	◐	B-	22	9.2	—	0.89	2500	638-5660
Kemper Inv. High-Yield		14,419	●	B	19	9.0	—[1][3]	1.89	1000	621-1048
Franklin AGE High-Income		14,258	●	B	18	9.3	4.00%	0.58	100	342-5236
IDS Extra Income		13,989	●	B-	20	8.9	5.00	0.83	2000	328-8300
MFS High-Income A		14,034	●	B-	19	8.7	4.75[1]	1.03	1000	225-2606
MetLife-State Street High-Inc. A		13,810	●	B-	22	9.1	4.50[1]	1.15	250	882-3302
▲ Three-month Treasury bills		11,834	◐	—	3	6.2	—	—	—	—
National Bond		14,492	●	B	NA	7.4	4.75[1]	1.38	2500	356-5535
Keystone Custodian B-4		13,583	●	B-	26	6.8	—[1][3]	2.09	1000	343-2898
First Investors Fund for Inc. [4]		12,956	●	B	18	6.4	6.90[1]	1.03	1000	423-4026
American Capital H.Y. Inv. A		13,050	●	B	19	5.8	4.75[1]	1.05	500	421-5666
United High-Income		12,435	●	B	18	5.2	8.50	0.76	500	366-5465
Dean Witter High-Yield Sec.		12,905	●	B-	31	2.3	5.50	0.77	1000	869-3863

GOVERNMENT

Fund name	Score (0–100)	5 years	Risk	Quality	Performance '93	Performance '88–'92	Load	Expense	Minimum	Phone 800-
Fidelity Government Securities		$13,781	○	AAA	12%	10.4%	—	0.70%	$2500	544-8888
Vanguard F.I. Short-Term Fed.		13,081	◐	AAA	7	8.9	—	0.27	3000	662-7447
Government Income Securities		13,159	◐	AAA	5	9.4	1.00%[5]	0.90	1500	245-5051
Investors Trust U.S. Gov. Secs. B		13,302	◐	AAA	8	9.7	—[1][3]	1.64	1500	656-6626
SunAmerica U.S. Gov. Secs. B		12,636	●	AAA	4	8.1	—[1][3]	1.82	500	858-8850
Delaware Treasury Res. Int.		12,606	●	AAA	5	8.1	3.00[1]	0.87	1000	523-4640

Fund name	Score	5 years	Risk	Quality	Performance '93	Performance '88-'92	Load	Expense	Minimum	Phone 800-
Dean Witter U.S. Gov. Secs.		12,997	◐	AAA	6	8.6	—[1][3]	1.20	1000	869-3863
Prudential Government Plus B		13,243	○	AAA	7	9.4	—[1][3]	1.69	1000	225-1852
Merrill Lynch Fed. Securities A		12,885	◐	AAA	7	9.3	4.00[1]	0.80	1000	637-3863
Dean Witter Federal Securities		13,336	○	AAA	8	9.4	—[1][3]	1.48	1000	869-3863
U.S. Government Securities		12,897	◐	AAA	10	8.9	4.75[1]	0.88	1000	421-0180
Vanguard F.I. Long-Term Trsry.		13,921	●	AAA	17	11.4	—	0.27	3000	662-7447
Fund for U.S. Gov. Securities A		12,679	◐	AAA	5	8.8	4.50	0.84	500	245-5051
Smith Barney Shearson Gov. Sec. B		13,417	○	AAA	11	10.0	—[1][3]	1.71	1000	451-2010
Lord Abbett U.S. Gov. Secs.		13,140	◐	AAA	9	9.6	4.75[1]	0.87	500	874-3733
Twentieth Century U.S. Gov.		12,594	○	AAA	4	7.8	—	0.99	1000	345-2021
American Capital Gov. Secs. A		13,058	◐	AAA	8	9.5	4.75[1]	0.97	500	421-5666
Fortis U.S. Gov. Securities		12,767	○	AAA	8	8.9	4.50	0.72	500	800-2638
Kemper Investment Gov.		13,117	◐	AAA	5	8.7	—[1][3]	1.86	1000	621-1048
Three-month Treasury bills		11,834	●	—	3	6.2	—	—	—	—
MainStay Government		12,774	○	AAA	6	8.3	—[1][2]	1.80	500	522-4202
Putnam Federal Income		12,782	○	AAA	5	8.8	4.75[1]	1.11	500	225-1581
Colonial Federal Securities A		12,729	○	AAA	12	8.9	4.75[1]	1.26	1000	248-2828
Transamerica Gov. Securities		12,799	◐	AAA	8	8.5	4.75[1]	1.53	1000	343-6840
Putnam American Gov. Income		12,111	○	AAA	6	7.2	4.75[1]	0.96	500	225-1581

GOVERNMENT: Mortgage

Fund name	Score (0 25 50 75 100)	5 years	Risk	Quality	Performance '93	Performance '88-'92	Load	Expense	Minimum	Phone 800-
Vanguard F.I. GNMA		$13,982	○	AAA	6%	11.4%	—	0.29%	$3000	662-7447
Benham GNMA Income		13,869	◐	AAA	7	11.0	—	0.57	1000	472-3389
Fidelity Ginnie Mae		13,579	◐	AAA	6	10.4	—	0.81	2500	544-8888
T. Rowe Price GNMA		13,599	◐	AAA	6	10.2	—	0.80	2500	638-5660
Scudder GNMA		13,632	○	AAA	6	10.3	—	0.94	1000	225-2470

[1] 12b-1 fee. [2] Redemption fee if you sell within one year. [3] Deferred sales charge. [4] Closed to new investors at time of study. [5] Redemption fee when you sell. [6] Adjusted for 28% federal tax bracket.

GOVERNMENT: MORTGAGE Continued

Fund name	Score (0–100)	5 years	Risk	Quality	Performance '93	Performance '88-'92	Load	Expense	Minimum	Phone 800-
Alliance Mortgage Sec. Inc. A		$13,383	◗	A	10%	10.1%	3.00% ①	1.20%	$250	227-4618
Dreyfus GNMA		13,387	◗	AAA	7	9.7	— ①	0.94	2500	645-6561
Franklin U.S. Gov. Securities		13,100	◗	AAA	7	9.6	4.00	0.53	100	342-5236
Fidelity Mortgage Securities		13,272	◗	AAA	7	9.8	—	0.78	2500	544-8888
Franklin Tax-Adv. U.S. Gov.		13,130	◗	AAA	8	9.7	4.00	0.67	2500	342-5236
Smith Barney U.S. Gov. Sec. A		13,247	○	AAA	6	10.1	4.00	0.50	3000	544-7835
Liberty Financial U.S. Gov.		12,734	◑	AAA	6	8.4	4.50 ①	0.82	500	872-5426
Franklin Adj. U.S. Gov. Secs.		12,174	◖●	AAA	1	7.3	2.25 ①	0.34	100	342-5236
Van Kampen Merritt U.S. Gov.		12,992	○	AAA	8	9.5	4.90 ①	0.77	1500	225-2222
PaineWebber U.S. Gov. Inc. A		12,991	◑	AAA	7	9.3	4.00 ①	0.93	1000	647-1568
IDS Federal Income		12,444	◑	AAA	6	8.3	5.00	0.77	2000	328-8300
Putnam U.S. Gov. Income A		12,645	◗	AAA	6	8.7	4.75 ①	1.01	500	225-1581
Smith Barney Shearson Man. Gov. A		12,945	○	AAA	9	9.0	4.50 ①	0.82	1000	451-2010
Kemper U.S. Gov. Securities		12,954	○	AAA	6	9.3	4.50	0.64	1000	621-1048
Prudential GNMA B		12,963	○	AAA	4	8.4	— ① ③	1.60	1000	225-1852
▲ Three-month Treasury bills		11,834	●	—	3	6.2	—	—	—	—
Colonial U.S. Government A		12,246	◗	AAA	6	7.6	4.75 ①	1.09	1000	248-2828
MFS Lifetime Gov. Mortgage		12,639	◑	AAA	NA	7.8	— ① ③	1.95	1000	225-2606
Putnam Adj. Rate U.S. Gov. A		11,727	◖●	AAA	0	5.9	3.25 ①	1.12	500	225-1581
MFS Government Mortgage A		12,262	○	AAA	7	7.6	4.75 ①	1.42	1000	225-2606

MUNICIPAL

Fund name	Score	5 years	Risk	Quality	Performance '93	Performance '88-'92	Load	Expense	Minimum	Phone 800-
Vanguard Municipal High-Yield		$13,733	○	A	13%	11.0%	—	0.23%	$3000	662-7447
USAA Tax-Exempt Long-Term		13,332	○	AA	13	10.1	—	0.39	3000	382-8722
Fidelity High-Yield Tax-Free		13,281	◑	BB	13	10.1	—	0.56	2500	544-8888
Vanguard Muni. Insured L. Term		13,455	○	AAA	13	10.4	—	0.23	3000	662-7447
Vanguard Municipal Int.-Term		13,284	○	AA	12	9.6	—	0.23	3000	662-7447
Dreyfus Municipal Bond		13,159	○	A	13	9.5	—	0.68	2500	645-6561
Dreyfus Int. Municipal Bond		13,006	○	A	12	8.7	—	0.71	2500	645-6561
T. Rowe Price Tax-Free Income		13,137	○	AA	13	8.9	—	0.61	2500	638-5660
Eaton Vance National Muni.		13,004	○	BB	15	8.6	—[1][3]	1.79	1000	225-6265
Franklin Fed. Tax-Free Income		12,861	○	A	11	9.3	4.00%	0.51	100	342-5236
Franklin High-Yld. Tax-Free Inc.		12,738	◑	B	13	9.1	4.00	0.53	100	342-5236
Franklin Insured Tax-Free Inc.		12,744	○	AAA	12	9.1	4.00	0.53	100	342-5236
Putnam Tax Exempt Income A		12,845	○	AA	13	9.3	4.75	0.66	500	225-1581
Merrill Lynch Muni. Insured A		12,759	○	AAA	13	8.8	4.00	0.44	1000	637-3863
Smith Barney Shearson Man. Muni. A		12,785	○	A	16	8.9	4.50	0.59	1000	451-2010
Merrill Lynch Muni. National A		12,682	○	A	13	8.7	4.00	0.55	1000	637-3863
Dean Witter Tax-Exempt Sec.		12,707	○	A	11	9.1	4.00	0.49	1000	869-3863
Kemper Municipal Bond		12,716	◑	AA	13	8.6	4.50	0.48	1000	621-1048
MFS Municipal Bond A		12,738	◑	AA	14	8.9	4.75	0.57	1000	225-2606
IDS High-Yield Tax-Exempt		12,501	◑	BBB	11	8.3	5.00	0.62	2000	328-8300
Colonial Tax-Exempt A		12,398	◑	A	9	7.9	4.75[1]	1.05	1000	248-2828
Nuveen Municipal Bond		12,414	◑	AA	10	8.2	4.75	0.59	1000	351-4100
First Inv. Insured Tax-Exempt		11,998	◑	AAA	13	7.3	6.90[1]	1.16	1000	423-4026
IDS Tax-Exempt Bond		12,188	○	AA	13	7.6	5.00	0.64	2000	328-8300
▲ Three-month Treasury bills [6]		11,321	●	—	3	6.2	—	—	—	—

[1] 12b-1 fee. [2] Redemption fee if you sell within one year. [3] Deferred sales charge. [4] Closed to new investors at time of study. [5] Redemption fee when you sell. [6] Adjusted for 28% federal tax bracket.

Data source: Morningstar, Inc.

GLOSSARY OF COMMON MUTUAL FUND TERMS

The world of investing has a language all its own, a language that may sometimes seem only distantly related to English. This chapter translates some of the terms you're likely to encounter in reading about and shopping for mutual funds. The most basic terms—the ones we think belong in any fund investor's portfolio of knowledge—are marked with an asterisk (*). The other terms are either more technical or of narrower interest. (For more detailed explanations of the various types of mutual funds, see chapter 2.)

*Asked Price   Also called ask price, buy price, or offer price, this figure represents how much it would cost to buy one share of a particular mutual fund, including any sales charges. Some newspaper listings of mutual funds show each fund's asked price and net asset value (usually abbreviated as NAV) in side-by-side columns. The difference between the two columns reflects the sales charge, if any. For funds that don't impose a sales charge (no-load funds), the columns may be the same, or one column will show the abbreviation NL.

*Asset Allocation   An investing strategy that involves divvying up assets among investments such as stocks, bonds, real estate, "cash," and precious metals, according to a formula that may vary with market conditions. Some funds follow an asset-allocation strategy. Investors can also do their own asset allocation by investing in a number of different types of funds.

*Assets   The total value of a mutual fund's holdings. Though this figure is often included in ratings of mutual funds to give investors an idea of the relative sizes of funds, it says little about a fund beyond how much investor money it has managed to attract. Some fund watchers have advanced the theory that funds with immense assets are more difficult to manage than smaller funds and therefore less likely to be top performers—just as an ocean liner tends to be less maneuverable than a speedboat. Yet there always seem to be funds, both large and small, that somehow defy that logic.

Average Maturity   A measure of the length of time, on average, until the various holdings in a fund's portfolio repay their principal and stop paying interest. A bond mutual fund, for example, may own hundreds of bonds that mature at different points in the future. The average maturity of a fund's portfolio is useful in comparing bond funds, particularly those that claim to follow the same basic investment strategy. A bond fund with a higher average maturity should generally pay a higher rate of interest at any given time, because the further in the future a bond matures, the more risk it is subject to in the meantime. Average maturity is also referred to as average *weighted* maturity. Weighting takes into account the portion of a fund's assets that is invested in bonds of various maturities. The more money the fund has invested in a particular bond, the more the maturity of that bond will count for in determining the fund's average maturity. (For more about bond funds and the risks associated with them, see chapter 2.)

*Back-end Load   Also known as a deferred sales charge or deferred sales load, this is a charge that some funds impose when shares are sold. Some funds impose back-end sales charges that disappear after a certain number of years. (See also Contingent deferred sales charge, Load, and Redemption fee.)

Backup Withholding   An Internal Revenue Service requirement that generally affects only investors who failed to report interest and dividends in the past or who didn't provide their Social Security number when they opened a mutual fund account. Under backup withholding, the fund will withhold 20 percent of all payments to the investor; the investor can then claim that amount as federal income tax withheld on Form 1040. If you are not subject to backup withholding, you will be required to sign a statement to that effect when you make your initial investment in a fund.

Basis Point   A unit of measure you're most likely to see in reading about the yields on bond or money-market mutual funds. One basis point equals 0.01 percent. A money-market fund yielding 4.30 percent, for example, is said to be returning 30 more basis points than a fund yielding 4.00 percent.

Bear Market   A prolonged period of declining stock or bond prices. Investors who are pessimistic about the future prospects of an investment are said to be "bearish" about it. (See also Bull market.)

Beta   A commonly used risk measure that compares a fund's volatility (up or down) to that of a market index, such as the S&P 500 stock market index. The higher the number, the more volatile a fund is expected to be. A fund with a beta of 1.00 is said to match the market index in terms of its volatility.

*Bid Price   Also called redemption price, it's the price at which a mutual fund company will buy back your shares. In general, the bid price is the same as the net asset value.

Blue Chip   Wall Street slang, borrowed from poker, for stocks of large, stable companies with long records of reliable, if not spectacular, earnings and dividends. Examples of blue chip companies, circa 1993, are Coca-Cola, General Electric, and Maytag.

*Bond   Essentially, an IOU of a corporation or a government. Bonds either pay interest at set intervals or sell at a discount to their face value—in effect, paying interest when they mature. Bonds come in many different varieties, including corporate, government, and municipal. They also come in many different maturities; short-, intermediate-, and long-term are the most commonly used categories.

Bond Rating   Any of a number of systems for determining the likelihood that a bond issuer will repay its debt. Well-known bond raters include Moody's and Standard & Poor's (S&P). Their publications are often available at public libraries.

Bull Market   The opposite of a bear market, a prolonged period of rising stock or bond prices. Optimistic investors are said to be "bullish."

*Buy-and-Hold   An investing strategy for people who believe in the long-term prospects of a mutual fund or other investment and aren't unduly alarmed by its short-term ups and downs. The opposite strategy is called market timing.

*Buy Price   Sometimes shortened in newspaper listings and elsewhere to "buy." (See Asked price.)

*Capital Gain   The difference between what you paid for a share of a mutual fund (or other investment) and what you sold it for—assuming you didn't lose money in the process.

*Capital-Gains Distribution   Periodically, mutual funds distribute to their shareholders any profits they have made in selling securities. Distributions usually occur once a year, often in December. Investors may receive their distributions in the form of a check or have them automatically reinvested in the fund to buy more shares. You should try to avoid investing immediately before a capital-gains distribution, especially if a large sum of money is involved. Otherwise, you'll end up owing tax on a profit that you didn't enjoy, unless the money is in a tax-deferred account. (See chapter 7.)

Cash   In the investment world, cash refers not only to what most of us carry in our wallets but also to so-called cash equivalents, such as short-term bank CDs and short-term government securities. When a stock mutual fund has a large cash position, that often means its manager has sold part of its stock portfolio in anticipation of a market decline (and in hopes of an opportunity to buy stocks at a lower price). Some funds remain fully invested in the stock market, except for a small cash reserve they maintain to buy back shares from investors redeeming shares. Other funds, particularly those whose managers practice market timing, may have dramatically fluctuating cash positions, depending on where they see the market heading.

Closed-end Fund Also called closed-end investment company. A type of fund that issues a fixed number of shares that trade on a stock exchange much like stocks. Closed-end funds often invest in the securities of foreign companies and governments. Unlike open-end funds, closed-end funds may sell for more or less than the market value of the securities they hold, depending on demand for them. When that happens they are said to be selling at a premium, or at a discount.

Commercial Paper A short-term loan to a corporation. Money-market funds and short-term bond funds may hold commercial paper from many corporations.

*Common Stock A share of ownership in a corporation. (See also Preferred stock.)

*Contingent Deferred Sales Charge A fee that some funds charge if you sell your fund shares within a certain number of years. (See also Back-end load.)

Contractual Plan Also called a periodic payment plan, this is a contract with a mutual fund company in which an investor agrees to invest a certain amount each year for a set number of years. Such plans usually have very high sales charges at the outset. Investors can achieve much the same result—without the punishing sales charges—by practicing dollar-cost averaging in a no-load mutual fund.

*Conversion Also known as an exchange or, more commonly, a switch, conversion is the act of trading shares in one mutual fund for shares in another fund within the same family. Procedures vary from fund company to fund company, as do the rules on how many conversions companies allow during a given time period. Keep in mind that each conversion is considered a taxable event by the IRS. That is, any profit you make in redeeming the shares of the fund you switch out of will be counted as taxable income for that year, even though you only moved money from one account to another.

Convertibles More formally known as convertible securities, convertibles are usually corporate bonds or preferred stocks that can be exchanged for common stock at an agreed-upon price. They are of interest mostly to investors looking for income. Some mutual funds primarily hold convertible securities; others include them as part of a more diversified portfolio.

*Cost Basis The amount paid for fund shares, used in determining gain or loss for tax purposes. If shares are bought through a dividend reinvestment plan, and taxes have already been paid on those dividends, that amount should be added to the cost basis to avoid being taxed twice on the same income.

*Current Yield The annual dividends that a fund is currently paying, shown as a percentage of its current share price.

Custodial Fee A charge that funds impose, usually annually, to reimburse the custodians of certain accounts, such as Individual Retirement Accounts.

Custodian The financial institution, such as a bank, that holds a mutual fund's securities and cash for safekeeping.

Debenture An obligation much like a bond, except that it is not backed by any specific collateral, only the issuer's credit.

Debt An obligation to repay a loan. As an investor, you're also likely to see it used as a synonym for bonds in magazine and newspaper articles about mutual funds. Substitute the word "bonds" for the word "debt" (or for the even more stilted "debt instruments"), and you'll usually know what the writer had in mind.

Discount A term you may encounter in reading about closed-end funds. Shares in closed-end mutual funds sometimes sell for less than the fund's net asset value per share because of market supply and demand. At those times they are said to be selling at a discount. When closed-end funds sell at prices greater than their net asset value per share, they are said to be selling at a premium.

Distributions   Payments made by a fund to shareholders from capital gains, interest, or dividends. Shareholders can receive distributions in the form of a check or have them automatically reinvested to buy more fund shares. Either way, distributions are taxable income and have to be reported on your tax return, unless they're in a tax-deferred account.

Diversification   The familiar concept of "not putting all of your eggs in one basket." Diversification is the most touted advantage of mutual funds over other investments such as individual stocks—and not without reason. A typical mutual fund owns dozens, perhaps hundreds, of different securities, so the failure of any one of them would have a small effect on the value of the overall portfolio. Just as mutual funds practice diversification, so should fund investors, by not putting all of their money into one fund. (See chapter 4.)

*Dividend   Money that a corporation pays its shareholders, usually quarterly, based on the number of shares they own. Mutual funds receive dividends from stocks they own. Funds also pay dividends to their shareholders. Money market and bond funds usually pay them monthly; stock funds, every three months, every six months, or once a year.

*Dividend Reinvestment Plan   Sometimes known by its initials (DRP), this is a convenient arrangement you can make with a mutual fund company to have your dividends automatically reinvested to buy more shares (or partial shares). Note that reinvested dividends are taxed just as if you had received the money in cash. Note also that a small number of mutual fund companies impose sales charges on reinvested dividends—a nervy practice, at best.

*Dollar-Cost Averaging   An investment technique that suggests investing the same dollar amount at set intervals, such as once a month. Your money will buy more fund shares when prices are low and fewer shares when prices are high, resulting in a lower average share price overall. (See chapter 3.)

Equity   The opposite of debt; something you own. You may also encounter the term "equities" used as a synonym for stocks.

*Exchange   In mutual fund parlance, the trading of shares in one fund for shares in another fund in the same family. (See Conversion.)

Exchange Fee   The fee that some funds impose when you transfer money from one fund to another within that fund family. Exchange fees, if any, are noted in each fund's prospectus. Take particular note of them if you plan to move money between accounts frequently.

Ex-dividend   The period between the date when a fund announces a dividend and the date that dividend is paid. Investors who buy fund shares during this period do not receive the dividend when it is paid.

Ex-dividend Date   The date on which a fund's net asset value drops to reflect the payment of a dividend. Most newspaper listings of mutual funds will note that with an X or an XD after the fund's name or next to its net asset value.

Expense Ratio   The percentage of a fund's net assets siphoned off by the fund company to pay for expenses. Take an especially hard look at expense ratios when shopping among bond funds, because high expenses can quickly diminish a bond fund's return.

First In/First Out   The most common method of determining the cost basis of shares you sold for tax purposes. The first-in/first-out, or FIFO, method assumes that you sold the shares you held for the longest time. Because fund shares should increase in value over time, this method is likely to result in a lower cost basis—and a higher tax—than some other methods for figuring your cost basis. (The various methods are explained in chapter 6.)

Fixed-Income   Another synonym for bonds. "Fixed" refers to the fact that bonds promise to pay a predictable rate of interest, or income, until they mature. Bond funds often are referred to as fixed-income funds, although that can be deceptive. In periods of rising or falling interest rates, the income that bond funds pay may fluctuate, as older holdings mature and fund managers have to buy new issues for their portfolios. When the rates on newly issued bonds are falling, fund managers may have to either reduce dividend payments to investors or return part of investors' principal as monthly income. (See also Total return and Yield.)

Front-end Load   See Load.

Fund Family   An investment company offering a number of different mutual funds with different goals. A family usually consists of at least several stock and bond funds and a money-market fund. (For advice on choosing fund families and getting the best service from them, see chapter 8.)

Global   In the language of mutual funds, global usually means all the countries on the world globe including the United States. By contrast, international means all the world except the United States. (See chapter 2.)

Growth   A term you'll frequently see in the ads and sales literature of stock funds. It also appears in the names of many funds. Growth generally refers to stocks with the potential of increasing in share price as the companies behind them expand and prosper. Such companies may not pay stock dividends but instead reinvest their profits in research and development. (See chapter 2.)

High-Yield Bond   More commonly known as a "junk bond." High-yield bonds are issued by companies whose prospects are considered more risky than those of mainstream companies. High-yield bonds promise to pay a slightly higher rate of interest to compensate investors for taking that greater risk. Some funds invest almost entirely in high-yield bonds; many others include them as part of their portfolios.

Income   When used in connection with stock funds, income refers to companies that pay high dividends rather than those whose share price is likely to appreciate greatly (see Growth). Funds with income as their objective may invest in some combination of dividend-paying stocks and bonds.

Index   A statistical model designed to measure the performance of an investment market. Among the better known indexes are the Standard & Poor's 500 stock index, the Wilshire 5000 stock index, and the Salomon Brothers bond index. There are also more specialized indexes, sometimes referred to as subindexes, that measure the performance of different sectors of the market, such as health-care or financial-services stocks.

*Index Fund   A fund that buys all (or a representative sample) of the stocks or bonds that make up one of the widely known market indexes, with the goal of mirroring the performance of that index. The theory behind index funds is simple: Since most funds in a given year fail to outperform the market, why not simply buy the market? Index funds tend to lag behind their chosen index at least slightly, because they have expenses and indexes do not. But their expenses tend to be less than those of more actively managed mutual funds.

International   A term that typically refers to funds that invest in countries other than the United States. (See Global.)

Investment Adviser   A firm employed by a mutual fund to advise it on investing decisions. The adviser may be an independent firm or a subsidiary of the investment company offering that mutual fund. Some funds may have more than one adviser. (See Management fee.)

Investment Company   A firm that operates a mutual fund or a family of mutual funds. The principal law governing mutual funds is the Investment Company Act of 1940.

*Investment Objective   The goal of a mutual fund—such as capital appreciation or regular income—and the type of securities it invests in, as spelled out in its prospectus. As part of its objective, the fund may also describe the investment tactics its managers plan to follow.

Junk Bond   See High-yield bond.

Leverage   Using borrowed money to buy securities. Some funds practice leveraging in an attempt to boost their returns.

*Liquidity   A rough measure of how quickly a particular asset can be turned into cash. Most mutual funds are highly liquid, because their shares can be redeemed immediately or within a few days, depending on the redemption method used. Many money-market funds offer checkwriting privileges, making them as liquid as a checking account at a bank.

Load   A commission, typically in the form of a percentage, that investors must pay to buy or sell certain mutual funds. The former are known as front-end loads or sales charges, the latter as back-end loads. Loads are often used to pay the stockbroker or financial planner who steers a client toward a particular fund. Funds that do not impose loads are called no-loads or pure no-loads.

Low-Load Fund   A front-end load that is generally in the 1 to 3 percent range.

Maintenance Fee   See Custodial fee.

Management Fee   Money paid by the mutual fund to its investment advisers, usually expressed as a percentage of the fund's assets. Management fees across the fund industry recently averaged about one-half of 1 percent of assets, according to the Investment Company Institute, the fund industry's trade group. Management fees are listed in a fund's prospectus under the heading Fund Expenses.

Manager   The man, woman, or committee whose job it is to make the investment decisions for a particular mutual fund. Also known as a portfolio manager or money manager.

Margin Account   An account with a brokerage firm that allows an investor to borrow on the securities already in the account (such as mutual funds) to buy more securities, subject to certain legal limits. Buying on margin, as this practice is called, is a risky business suitable only for very sophisticated investors.

Market Timing   An investment strategy based on guessing which way the market is headed. Ideally, a market timer would be able to sell stocks just as they reached their peak and buy stocks once they hit bottom and start back up again. Market timers look at a variety of statistical indicators in making their decisions. Their results over the years have been mixed. Some mutual funds practice market timing by moving money from stocks to bonds or "cash," when they think the market is poised for a fall. Many mutual fund shareholders do the same thing by moving from stock funds to bond or money-market funds when they fear a decline. The opposite approach to market timing is known as buy-and-hold.

Maturity   The date on which a bond is scheduled to pay back its principal. Bond funds, which may own many dozens of different bonds, show the maturity of each one in their lists of holdings. The collective maturity of those bonds is referred to as the fund's average maturity.

*Minimum Initial Investment   How much money you must put into a fund at the outset, typically under $5,000, and sometimes as low as $1. Many funds with otherwise high minimums set lower minimums for Individual Retirement Accounts. Some funds also set minimums, such as $100, for subsequent investments to existing accounts.

Municipal Bond   A bond issued by a state or local government or by a government agency. Municipal bond funds have certain tax advantages over other types of bond funds. (See chapter 6.)

Mutual Fund Complex   Another name for a fund family.

NASDAQ   Pronounced Naz-dak, the abbreviation for the National Association of Securities Dealers Automated Quotations system. NASDAQ is a computerized system for trading over-the-counter and other securities.

Net Asset Value Per Share (NAV)   The value of one share of a mutual fund, determined each day by dividing the total assets of the fund (minus any liabilities) by the number of shares outstanding. For no-load funds, the net asset value is the price you would pay to buy a share. For funds with loads, the price is determined by adding the load to the net asset value. (See Asked price.)

NL   An abbreviation for no-load fund used in some newspaper listings of mutual funds.

No-load   A fund that doesn't impose front-end sales charges when you buy shares or back-end sales charges when you sell them. No-loads generally are sold directly to investors rather than through a broker. Pure no-loads do not impose 12b-1 fees.

Note   A written agreement to pay a specified amount by a certain date, typically issued by a corporation or a government. It's much like a bond, except that it may pay interest at maturity rather than at specific intervals and it may mature sooner. Bond mutual funds may hold notes as well as bonds and other securities.

Objective   See Investment objective.

Offer Price   See Asked price.

Open-end Fund   What most people today probably think of when they think of a mutual fund. Open-end funds issue shares to meet investor demand (thus, the total number of shares is "open"). The value of their shares is determined by dividing the fund's total net assets by the number of shares outstanding.

Option   The right to buy or sell a security such as a certain corporation's stock at a specified price for a specified period of time. Options that are not used ("exercised" in financial jargon) expire and become worthless. Some mutual fund managers use options to protect their portfolios from unexpected swings in a stock's price; others speculate in options as a way to increase their fund's total return.

Over-the-Counter (OTC) Stocks   Typically the shares of small, new companies, OTC stocks don't trade on exchanges, but through a telephone or computer network of dealers. Some aggressive-growth mutual funds specialize in OTC stocks; others hold them as a small portion of their portfolios. (See NASDAQ.)

Portfolio   The holdings of a mutual fund. Also, your own holdings of mutual funds.

Portfolio Manager   See Manager.

Preferred Stock   Like common stock, preferred stock represents a share of ownership in a corporation. It differs from common stock, in that its holders have a greater claim on dividends and on the company's assets if the company gets into trouble. Many mutual funds hold a small percentage of preferred stocks in their portfolios.

Premium A term from the world of closed-end funds, referring to funds that sell for more than their assets are currently worth.

Prepayment Risk A danger to investors in mortgage-backed mutual funds, such as Ginnie Mae funds. When interest rates fall, many homeowners will refinance their mortgages. When the older mortgages are paid off early, the fund will have to reinvest that money at the prevailing lower rates and reduce its interest payments to shareholders.

Price-Earnings Ratio A common measure of how expensive or inexpensive a stock is, often referred to simply as P/E. You're likely to encounter it in reading about a stock fund's investment objectives. A price-earnings ratio is determined by dividing the current price of one share of a stock by the company's annual earnings per share. (Earnings per share represents the company's after-tax profits divided by the number of outstanding shares.) A company with a share price of $25 that reported earnings of $1.47 per share would have a P/E of 17 ($25 divided by $1.47 equals 17). A $12.50 stock that also earned $1.47 would have a P/E of 8.5. The higher a stock's P/E, the more expensive it is considered, because investors must pay more money for its earnings than they would for a stock with a lower share price but identical earnings. An equity-income stock fund, for example, may own more stocks with low P/E ratios, because its main objective is a high rate of income. An aggressive-growth fund, by contrast, may own more high P/E stocks, because its goal is to invest in companies with the best prospects for rapid future growth. Such companies may have little or no profit to report now because, for example, they're investing heavily in research and development, making their P/E ratios high. It's also possible to determine the P/E ratio for an entire mutual fund by averaging the ratios of all the stocks it owns and taking into account how large a percentage of the total portfolio each stock represents.

Prospectus A booklet that describes a fund's investment objectives, performance record, fees, and services to investors. A no-load fund must send you a prospectus before you invest and, if you do invest, periodically thereafter. If you buy a fund through a salesperson, you may receive a prospectus only when the sale is completed.

Proxy   Written authorization for someone to cast your vote at a meeting of shareholders. Usually once a year, before the fund's annual meeting, you'll be asked to vote on certain matters, such as the election of the fund's board of directors and proposed changes in its investing policies or fee structures. Typically you'll be entitled to one vote for each share you own. Though shareholders in the past have tended to rubber-stamp whatever the fund's managers wanted, in recent years they have become more involved, particularly in voting down proposed fee increases.

Pure No-load   A fund that doesn't charge investors front-end loads, back-end loads, or 12b-1 fees. Some funds that refer to themselves as no-loads do impose 12b-1 fees.

Redemption   The selling of fund shares back to the fund. At some funds you can redeem shares by telephone; at others, a letter (and possibly a signature guarantee) will be required.

Redemption Fee   A fee some funds impose when shares are sold. Some funds charge redemption fees to discourage investors from selling shares too soon after buying them.

Return-of-Capital Distribution   A distribution you receive from a fund that represents a portion of the money you had invested to buy shares. A return-of-capital distribution shouldn't be confused with a capital-gains distribution. The latter represents a profit and is therefore taxable, while the former is simply a return of your own money and is not taxable. A return-of-capital distribution will affect the cost basis of your fund shares for tax purposes. (See chapter 6.)

Rollover   The process of moving money from one IRA to another or from an employee pension plan into an IRA. In a rollover, you can take possession of the money for up to 60 days. Another way to move IRA money is called an asset transfer. In a transfer, the money is moved directly from account to account without your taking possession of it. A recent change in the tax laws requires employers to withhold money when employees use a rollover to move money from an employer-sponsored retirement account into an IRA; for that reason, a direct transfer may be the better choice. (See chapter 5.)

Sales Charge   See Load.

Sector Fund   A mutual fund specializing in just one industry or sector of the economy, such as financial services, health care, or telecommunications. Sector funds sacrifice broad diversification—usually viewed as a virtue of mutual funds—to speculate on the fortunes of a narrow segment of the stock market. Predictably, some sector funds finish near the top of the charts for a given year, while others finish near the bottom. Sector funds are not for casual or risk-averse investors. Such funds are also referred to as specialized funds or specialized portfolios.

Security   A financial instrument such as a stock or a bond.

Selling Short   Also known as short selling, this is a speculative investment strategy practiced by some mutual fund managers. Here, in essence, is how it works: A fund manager who believes a certain stock is overpriced borrows shares of that stock from a broker and then sells them at the current market price. If the stock then falls in value, the fund manager can buy them back at the lower price, return them to the broker, and pocket the difference. If the stock rises in price, however, the fund manager will have to make up the difference.

Share   A single unit of ownership in a mutual fund or a corporation.

*Signature Guarantee   A requirement by some mutual fund companies that you have your signature authenticated by a bank officer or a brokerage firm before the fund will act on a letter from you to sell shares. This procedure can be a nuisance if you need your money in a hurry.

Small Cap   More formally known as a small-capitalization stock, this is the stock of a relatively small, usually new company with few shares outstanding. Small cap stocks are a favorite of aggressive-growth stock funds.

Statement of Additional Information   A supplement to a mutual fund prospectus, offering more detailed data about the fund.

*Switching   See Conversion.

*Total Return   A calculation of a fund's performance over a given period that takes into account both the rise and fall of its share price and any dividends or capital-gains distributions it has paid to investors. A fund's total return, compared with similar funds' returns, is the best single measure of a fund's performance. (See also Yield.)

Trade   To buy or sell fund shares.

Trade Date   The date on which a fund company sold you fund shares or bought them back from you. The price you pay or receive for your shares is determined by the closing net asset value on that day.

Trail Fee   A commission that a stockbroker or financial planner who sold you a mutual fund may receive each year that you stay in the fund. The point, obviously, is to give the salesperson an incentive to keep your money in that fund (with no effort on his or her part) rather than switch it to another fund in order to earn a fresh commission. Trail fees come out of the 12b-1 fee, if any, the fund charges you each year.

Transfer   See Conversion and Rollover.

Transfer Agent   An organization, typically a bank, that handles shareholder transactions and keeps records of them on behalf of a mutual fund.

TTY   Abbreviation for teletypewriter, a machine that allows people with hearing impairments to do business over the telephone with mutual fund companies. You may also see it referred to as a Telecommunications Device for the Deaf, or TDD. Many mutual fund companies now offer this service. (A list of some major ones, with their TTY numbers, appears in chapter 8.)

Turnover Ratio   The portion of a fund's securities that were sold and replaced by other securities during a one-year period. This figure is a rough indicator of how aggressive a portfolio manager is, though it says little about whether that aggressiveness translated into investment profits. A turnover ratio of 100 percent suggests that the fund replaced its entire portfolio over the course of a year. Aggressive stock funds may have turnover ratios well over 200 percent in a year. Even fairly mild-mannered stock funds may have turnover ratios in the 40 to 50 percent range. A fund's turnover ratio should be shown in the fund's prospectus. Funds with high turnover ratios are likely to produce more taxable capital gains than funds that don't trade as actively. So, given the choice of two funds with similar performance records, first consider the one with the lower turnover ratio. It should deliver a better after-tax return.

*12b-1 Fee   Named after a controversial section of a 1980 Securities and Exchange Commission ruling, the 12b-1 fee allows mutual fund companies to use a percentage of their (that is, their investors') assets to pay for advertising and marketing expenses. Typically, the percentage ranges from 0.25 to 0.75 percent. Called "hidden fees" by their detractors, 12b-1 fees are subtracted from a fund's share price before a shareholder ever sees them. You can find out whether a fund imposes 12b-1 fees by looking in its prospectus under the heading Fund Expenses.

Unit Trust   Also called a unit investment trust, a unit trust is something like a bond mutual fund, in that it invests in a large portfolio of income-producing securities and sells shares in that portfolio to investors. Unit trusts differ from mutual funds because their portfolios are fixed at the outset and tend not to change over time, except as their holdings mature or are called in. Some unit trusts specialize in securities such as tax-free municipal bonds or mortgage-backed bonds. In Great Britain, the term unit trust refers to an investment much like the open-end mutual fund in the United States.

Value   Like "growth," a term frequently seen in fund literature and in the names of some stock funds. Value generally refers to an investing strategy that seeks out stocks selling for less than they should be, given the corporation's soundness and its likelihood of paying future dividends. Such stocks are said to be "undervalued."

Value Averaging   A variation of dollar-cost averaging developed by Harvard business professor Michael E. Edleson in the late 1980s. In simple form it works like this: Rather than invest fixed amounts of money at specific intervals, as in dollar-cost averaging, the investor increases the value of his or her holdings by a fixed amount each interval. That means putting in more money when a fund account has fallen in value and less when it has risen. Value averaging promises a generally higher rate of return over time but obviously requires more attention on the part of the investor. So it's not for beginners or for people whose enthusiasm for monitoring their investments tends to come and go.

Variable Annuity   A contract with an insurance company in which the buyer's money is invested in a mutual fund in order to provide regular income at some future date. It's called variable because the amount of money the investor ultimately receives will depend on the performance of the mutual fund.

Variable Life Insurance   A life insurance policy that invests some or all of the policy's cash value in investments such as mutual funds.

Vesting   The process by which an employee gradually becomes eligible to receive a benefit funded by an employer. For example, you may be entitled to 20 percent of a retirement benefit after three years of work with your employer and another 20 percent for each additional year after that. At the end of seven years, you would be "fully vested" for 100 percent of the benefit. Note that with retirement plans funded by your own money, such as a 401(k) plan, you are immediately vested.

Volatility   The tendency for the price of a mutual fund or other investment to rise or fall over a short period of time. (See Beta.)

Warrant   A type of security that gives its owner the right to buy a certain amount of stock in the same company at a predetermined price. Some mutual funds will have a small part of their portfolio invested in warrants.

Wire Transfer   The movement of money electronically, such as from a mutual fund to your bank account or vice versa.

Yield   The annualized income paid by a fund to its investors, expressed as a percentage of share price. Yield doesn't convey whether a fund's shares have risen or fallen in value, so it can be deceptive. A fund may also prop up its yield for a time by returning a portion of investors' capital to them in the form of income. Though the investors will continue to receive a certain rate of income, the value of their shares will be eroding as a result. For these reasons, total return is a better overall measure of fund performance.

YTD   A frequently used abbreviation in mutual fund literature and performance tables, meaning year-to-date.

INDEX